Thomas a Kempis

Of the imitation of Christ in four books

A new translation

Thomas a Kempis

Of the imitation of Christ in four books
A new translation

ISBN/EAN: 9783741190629

Manufactured in Europe, USA, Canada, Australia, Japa

Cover: Foto ©Lupo / pixelio.de

Manufactured and distributed by brebook publishing software (www.brebook.com)

Thomas a Kempis

Of the imitation of Christ in four books

Library of Spiritual Works for English Catholics

Of the Imitation of Christ

RIVINGTONS

London .... Waterloo Place
Oxford .... High Street
Cambridge .... Trinity Street

(*All rights reserved*)

Library of Spiritual Works

FOR

English Catholics

OF THE

Imitation of Christ

IN FOUR BOOKS

BY

Thomas à Kempis

A New Translation

RIVINGTONS
London, Oxford, and Cambridge
MDCCCLXXV

CONTENTS.

BOOK I.

Chap.		Page
I.	Of the Imitation of Christ, and Contempt of the World and of all its Vanities	1
II.	Of Humility in respect to one's own Knowledge	3
III.	Of the Teaching of the Truth	5
IV.	Of Prudence in our Actions	9
V.	Of Reading the Scriptures	10
VI.	Of Inordinate Affections	11
VII.	Of Avoiding vain Hope and Self-esteem	12
VIII.	That excessive Familiarity should be Avoided	14
IX.	On Obedience and Subjection	15
X.	Of Talking too much	16
XI.	Of acquiring Peace, and of earnest Desire for growth in Grace	18
XII.	Of the Profitableness of Adversity	21
XIII.	Of Resisting Temptations	22
XIV.	Of Avoiding Rash Judgment	26
XV.	Of Works done from Charity	27
XVI.	On Bearing with the Defects of Others	29
XVII.	Of a Life apart from the World	31
XVIII.	Of the Examples of the Holy Fathers	32

CHAP.		PAGE
XIX.	On Religious Exercises	35
XX.	On the Love of Solitude and Silence	39
XXI.	Of Compunction of Heart	44
XXII.	Of the State of Human Misery	47
XXIII.	Of Meditation on Death	51
XXIV.	On Judgment, and the Punishments of Sinners	56
XXV.	Of Earnest Amendment of our Whole Life	61

BOOK II.

I.	Of the Inner Life	68
II.	Of Humble Submission	73
III.	Of a Good, Peaceful Man	74
IV.	Of a Pure Mind and a Simple Intention	76
V.	Of the Consideration of One's Self	78
VI.	Of the Joy of a Good Conscience	80
VII.	Of Loving Jesus above All Things	82
VIII.	Of Familiar Friendship with Jesus	84
IX.	Of the Absence of All Consolation	87
X.	Of Gratitude for the Grace of God	91
XI.	Of the Small Number of the Lovers of the Cross	94
XII.	Of the Royal Way of the Holy Cross	97

BOOK III.

I.	Of Christ's speaking inwardly to the Faithful Soul	106
II.	That Truth speaks inwardly without the sound of Words	107

CONTENTS

CHAP.		PAGE
III.	That the Words of God are to be Heard with Humility, and that many do not Ponder them	109
IV.	That we ought to Walk before God in Truth and Lowliness	113
V.	Of the wonderful Effect of Divine Love	115
VI.	Of the Test of a true Lover	120
VII.	Of hiding Grace under the guard of Humility	123
VIII.	Of a Low Estimation of one's self in the sight of God	127
IX.	That all things are to be referred to God, as to their Last End	129
X.	That to serve God, when you have Despised the World, is Sweet	130
XI.	That the Desires of the Heart are to be Examined and Restrained	133
XII.	Of cultivating Patience, and of striving against Lusts	135
XIII.	Of the Obedience of humble subjection after the Example of Jesus Christ	138
XIV.	Of the consideration of God's Secret Judgments, in order that we may not be Puffed up by any thing good in us	140
XV.	What we ought to Do or Say with regard to everything we Desire	142
XVI.	That True Comfort must be sought in God Alone	144
XVII.	That all Cares should be cast upon God	146
XVIII.	That temporal Miseries are to be borne patiently, after the Example of Christ	148
XIX.	On bearing Injuries, and of the proof of a truly Patient Man	150
XX.	Of the Acknowledgment of our own Infirmity; and of the Miseries of this Life	152

CHAP.		PAGE
XXI.	That we must find our Rest in God, above all good things and gifts	155
XXII.	Of the Remembrance of the many Benefits of God	159
XXIII.	Of Four Things which bring Great Peace .	162
XXIV.	Of Avoiding Curiosity and Inquisitiveness respecting the Lives of others . . .	165
XXV.	In what firm Peace of Heart and true Progress do consist	167
XXVI.	Of the Excellence of a Free Mind, which is gained more by humble Prayer than by Study	169
XXVII.	That it is Self-love which chiefly hinders us from obtaining the Supreme Good . . .	171
XXVIII.	Against the Tongues of Slanderers . .	173
XXIX.	How we ought to call upon God, and bless Him when we are in Trouble . . .	174
XXX.	Of Seeking Divine Assistance, and of Confidence in recovering Grace	176
XXXI.	Of Setting aside every Created Thing that the Creator may be found . . .	179
XXXII.	Of Self-denial and the Renunciation of every Corrupt Desire	182
XXXIII.	On the Changeableness of the Heart, and on directing our Final Intention towards God .	184
XXXIV.	That God is Sweet Above All and in All Things to him who loves Him . . .	186
XXXV.	That there is no Security from Temptation in this Life	188
XXXVI.	Against the vain Judgments of Men . .	190
XXXVII.	Of Pure and Entire Resignation of one's self for the obtaining Freedom of Heart . .	192
XXXVIII.	Of Ruling ourselves well as to the Outer Life, and of Recourse to God in Dangers . .	194

CHAP.		PAGE
XXXIX.	That a Man must not be over Eager about his Affairs	196
XL.	That a Man has nothing Good of Himself, nor any thing whereof to Glory	197
XLI.	Of the Contempt of all Worldly Honour	200
XLII.	That our Peace must not depend on Man	201
XLIII.	Against Vain and Worldly Learning	202
XLIV.	Of not taking up the Outward Things which come in our Path	204
XLV.	That we must not Trust every one, and that it is a common thing to Slip with the Tongue	206
XLVI.	Of Confidence in God when Words are Darted at us	209
XLVII.	That all Things, however grievous, are to be borne for the sake of Eternal Life	213
XLVIII.	On the Day of Eternity, and this Life's Distresses	215
XLIX.	Of the Desire of Eternal Life, and how great are the Rewards which are Promised to those who Strive for them	219
L.	How one in Desolation ought to Resign Himself into God's hands	224
LI.	That a Man must occupy himself with humble Works when he is unable to attain to Things which are Highest	229
LII.	That a Man ought to consider himself more worthy of Chastisement than of Consolation	230
LIII.	That the Grace of God does not mingle with the Worldly-minded	233
LIV.	Of the different Motions of Nature and Grace	235
LV.	On the Corruption of Nature, and the Efficacy of Divine Grace	240
LVI.	That we ought to Deny Ourselves, and to Imitate Christ by the Cross	244

CHAP.		PAGE
LVII.	That a Man should not be too Dejected at Failures or Trial	247
LVIII.	That Things beyond our reach, and the Secret Judgments of God, are not to be Scrutinized . .	249
LIX.	That all Hope and Trust is to be fixed in God Alone	255

BOOK IV.

I.	With how great Reverence Christ ought to be Received	258
II.	That the great Goodness and Love of God are made manifest to Man in this Sacrament . .	265
III.	That it is Profitable to Communicate often . .	269
IV.	That many Benefits are granted to those who Communicate Devoutly	272
V.	Of the Dignity of the Sacrament, and of the Priesthood	276
VI.	An Enquiry as to the Way to Prepare for Communion	279
VII.	Of the Examination of our own Conscience, and of the Resolution to Amend	279
VIII.	Of the Oblation of Christ on the Cross, and of Resignation of Ourselves	282
IX.	That we ought to Offer Ourselves and all that we have to God, and to Pray for All . . .	284
X.	That the Holy Communion is not for a Slight Thing to be Abstained from	287
XI.	That the Body and Blood of Christ and the Holy Scriptures are most necessary to the Faithful Soul	291
XII.	That he who is about to Communicate ought to use Great Diligence to Prepare himself for Christ .	296

CHAP.		PAGE
XIII.	That with the whole Heart the Devout Soul ought to seek Union with Christ in the Sacrament	299
XIV.	Of the ardent Desire of some Devout Persons for the Body and Blood of Christ	301
XV.	That the Grace of Devotion is obtained by Humility and Self-denial	303
XVI.	That we ought to lay open our Necessities to Christ, and to seek His Grace	305
XVII.	Of ardent Love for, and vehement Desire to Receive Christ	307
XVIII.	That a Man should not be a curious Searcher into the Sacrament, but a humble Follower of Christ, submitting his senses to the Sacred Faith	310

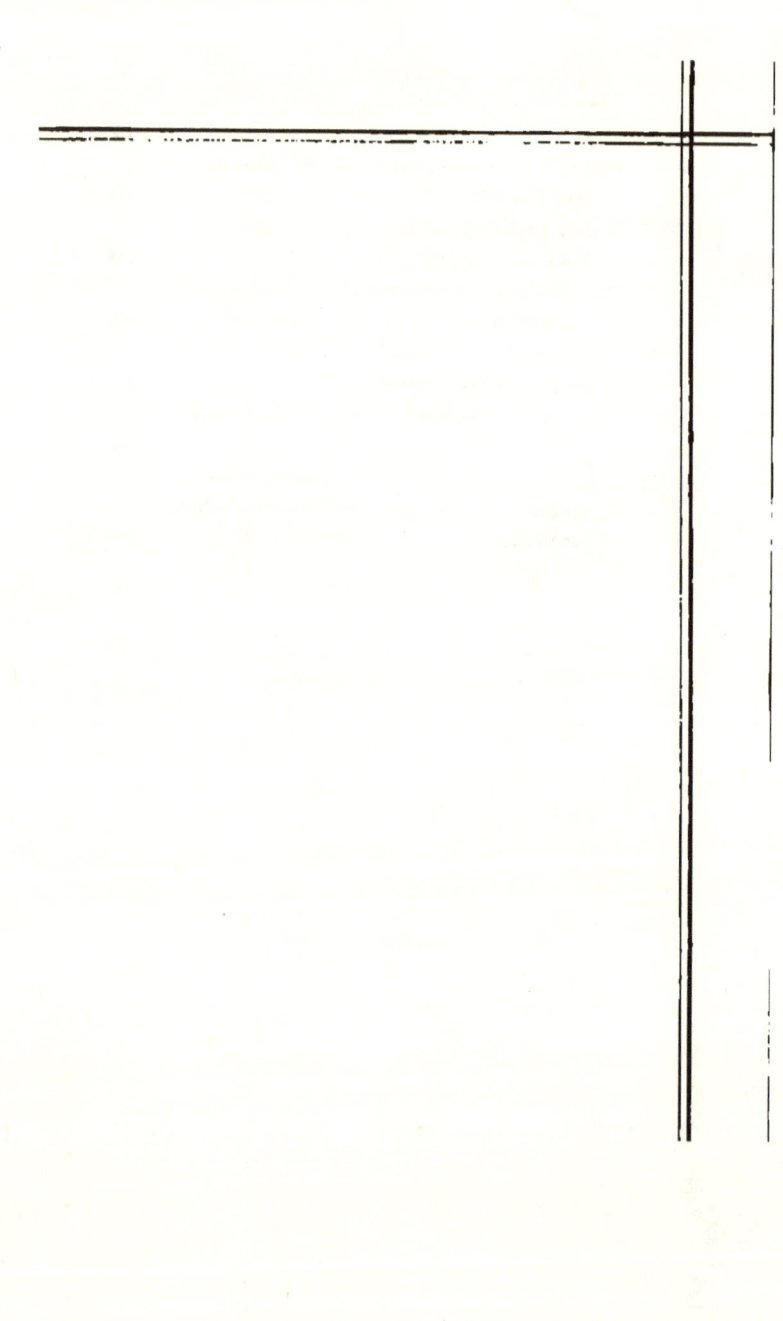

BOOK I.

CHAPTER I.

Of the Imitation of Christ, and Contempt of the World and of all its Vanities.

1. "HE that followeth Me shall not walk in darkness," saith the Lord. These are the words of Christ, by which we are reminded that we must copy His life and conduct, if we wish to be truly enlightened and to be delivered from all blindness of heart.

To meditate on the life of Jesus should therefore be our chief study.

2. His teaching surpasses all that the Saints have taught, and he who has the Spirit will find in it "the hidden manna."

But it happens that many, who often hear the Gospel, experience but little desire for it, because they do not possess the Spirit of Christ. For if you would completely and with delight enter into the meaning of Christ's words, you must take pains to bring your life into entire conformity with His.

3. What advantage is it to dispute profoundly about the doctrine of the Trinity, if by your lack of humility you are all the while displeasing the Trinity?

Surely sublime language does not render a man holy and just; but a virtuous life makes him dear to God.

I would rather feel compunction than know how to define it.

If you knew the whole Bible, and the maxims of all the philosophers, what would it profit you if you were destitute of the love of God and of His grace?

"Vanity of vanities; all is vanity," but to love God, and to serve Him solely.

This is the highest wisdom, when you despise the world in order to reach forth towards the Kingdom of Heaven.

4. It is vanity, therefore, to seek riches, and to trust in that which is perishable.

It is vanity, too, to seek for honours, and to strive for high positions.

It is vanity to follow the desires of the flesh, and to crave for that which would inevitably bring with it a sore punishment.

It is vanity to wish for length of life, and to care little that the life should be well spent.

It is vanity to think only of the present life, and not to provide for the future.

It is vanity to love that which swiftly passes away, and not to hasten onwards to that place where joy abides for ever.

5. Call frequently to your mind the saying of the Preacher—"The eye is not satisfied with seeing, nor the ear filled with hearing."

Strive, therefore, to withdraw your heart from the love of visible things, and to transfer your affections to things invisible; for, if you follow your sensual inclinations, you will stain your conscience, and lose the grace of God.

CHAPTER II.

Of Humility in respect to one's own Knowledge.

1. ALL men naturally desire knowledge; but what profit is there in knowledge without the fear of God.

Certainly, a lowly peasant who serves God is better than a proud philosopher, who, to the neglect of his own soul, studies the course of the heavens.

He who knows himself well, becomes vile in his own sight, and can take no delight in the praises of men.

If I knew all the things in the world, and were not in charity, what would it avail before God, Who will judge me by my actions.

2. Quiet that excessive desire for knowledge, because it brings with it much distraction and delusion.

Learned men are apt to wish to make a display of their learning, and to be spoken of as talented.

There are many things, the knowledge of which is of little or no use to the soul; and he is extremely foolish who turns his attention to such things, rather than to those which would be conducive to his salvation.

Many words do not satisfy the soul; but a good life calms the mind, and a pure conscience gives great confidence towards God.

3. The more you know and understand, the heavier will be your judgment, unless, in consequence of your greater knowledge, your life is a more holy one.

Wish not, then, to be extolled on account of your ability or learning, but rather regard the knowledge which is intrusted to you as a ground for apprehension.

If you fancy that you know many things, and fairly understand them; remember that the things you do not know are many more than those you know.

"Be not high-minded," but rather acknowledge your ignorance.

Why do you want to put yourself before others,

seeing there are many more learned than yourself, and more versed in the Law of God?

If you would know and learn anything profitably, love to be unknown, and to be regarded as of no account.

4. A true view of one's self, and consequently a low opinion of one's self, is the best and most valuable lesson to be acquired. To think nothing of one's self, and always to think well and highly of others, is great wisdom and perfectness.

If you were to see any one openly sin, or in the act of committing some crime, you ought not, therefore, to think the better of yourself.

We are all liable to fall, yet you should be convinced that there is no one more liable to do so than yourself.

CHAPTER III.

Of the Teaching of the Truth.

1. HAPPY is the man whom Truth directly teaches, not by means of figures and passing sounds, but as it really is in itself.

Our own opinion and our senses often deceive us, for we see but a little way into things.

What is the good of continually cavilling about hidden and abstruse matters, for our ignorance of which in the Day of Judgment we shall not be blamed?

It is a great folly to neglect what is useful and necessary, and of our own accord to inquire into what is curious and hurtful; having eyes we see not.

2. And why should we concern ourselves about logical distinctions?

He to whom the Eternal Word speaks is delivered from a multitude of disputes.

From the One Word proceed all things, and all things refer to Him, and He is "the Beginning" Who also speaks to us.

No one without Him can understand or rightly judge anything.

He who has but one aim, and refers all things to one principle, and views all things in one light, is able to abide steadfast, and to rest in God.

O God, the Truth, make me ever one with Thee in everlasting love!

It is a weariness to me to read and to hear many things; in Thee is all I want and desire.

Let all teachers be silent, and let the universe hold its peace in Thy Presence, and speak Thou only to me.

3. The more a man is undistracted and becomes inwardly simple, so much the more will he be able to enter easily into profound subjects; because his mind will be enlightened from above.

A pure, simple-minded, steadfast person is not distracted by the number of the things he has to do; because he does all for the glory of God, and is at rest in himself, and free from all self-seeking.

What hinders and vexes you more than the unmortified affections of your own heart?

A good and devout man first arranges in his own mind those duties which he has outwardly to perform; neither does he in the performance of them yield to the desires of a corrupt inclination, but regulates his actions by the dictates of sound reason.

Who has a sharper conflict than he who strives to conquer himself?

This must be our business, to conquer one's self, and to acquire more and more self-control daily, and to grow in virtue.

4. All perfection in this world has some imperfection coupled with it; and none of our investigations are without some obscurity.

A humble knowledge of yourself is a surer way to God than profound scientific research.

Learning, however, when considered in itself, or knowledge upon any subject, is not to be disparaged; for it is good, and ordained of God.

But what is meant is, that a good conscience and a virtuous life are always to be preferred to it.

Many strive to become learned more than to

become good; and the consequence is, they often go astray, and bring forth little or no results from their labours.

5. Oh, if men were as diligent in uprooting vices and planting virtues as they are in starting questions, there would not be so many evils and scandals in the world as there are, nor so much laxness amongst Religious persons.

Certainly when the Day of Judgment comes, we shall not be asked what we have read, but what we have done; not how well we have spoken, but how religiously we have lived.

Tell me, where are now all those Doctors and Masters with whom you were well acquainted whilst they were alive, and flourished in their pursuits?

Others fill their posts, and I dare say never think of them.

In their lifetime they seemed to be something, but now no one ever speaks of them.

6. Oh, how swiftly does this world's glory pass away! Would that their lives were in accordance with their knowledge, then would they have read and studied to some purpose!

How many in this world perish through vanity of learning, who care little for the service of God!

And because they wish rather to be esteemed great than to become lowly, therefore they become vain in their imaginations.

He is really great who is great in charity.

He is really great who is little in his own eyes, and cares not for the honour of high positions.

He is really wise who counts all earthly things as dung that he may win Christ.

He is really learned who does the Will of God, and forsakes his own will.

CHAPTER IV.

Of Prudence in our Actions.

1. WE must not trust every report or impulse, but cautiously and patiently ponder the matter in its relation to God.

Alas, such is our weakness, that we often more easily believe and repeat evil of others than good.

Those who are advanced in holiness do not at once give credit to every evil rumour; because they are conscious that human frailty makes men but too prone to relate evil, and to slip with the tongue.

2. It is great wisdom not to be hasty in action, nor to hold obstinately to one's own opinion; as also not to believe everything you hear, nor—even if you do believe it—at once to give it currency.

3. Seek advice from a man of wisdom and

judgment, and prefer to be instructed by those better informed than yourself rather than to follow your own devices.

A good life makes a man wise according to the estimate of God, and gives much experience. The more humble a man is in himself, and the more submissive to God, the more prudent and peaceful will he always become.

CHAPTER V.

Of Reading the Scriptures.

1. TRUTH must be sought in the Holy Scriptures and not eloquence.

The Bible ought always to be read with the assistance of the same Spirit by Whose agency it was written.

We should seek our profit when we read the Scriptures rather than subtle disputations.

We ought to be as ready to read a devotional book which is quite simple, as we are to read those which enter deeply and learnedly into their subjects.

Let not the authority of the writer, whether he be of high or low literary repute, influence you; but let the love of pure truth draw you to read.

You should not inquire who wrote it, but consider attentively what is written.

2. Men pass away; but "the truth of the Lord endureth for ever."

God speaks in various ways to us, without respect of persons.

Our curiosity often hinders us in reading the Scriptures, when we desire to look into and discuss those passages, when we should simply pass on.

If you wish to derive profit, read with lowliness, simplicity, and faith; and never covet a reputation for learning.

Be not reluctant to ask questions, and listen in silence to the words of holy persons; and do not dislike the parables of the ancients, for they are not quoted without cause.

CHAPTER VI.

Of Inordinate Affections.

1. WHENEVER a man inordinately desires anything, he instantly loses inward peace. The proud and covetous are never at rest, whilst the poor and lowly in spirit pass their life in continual peace.

The man who is not yet perfectly dead to self is quickly tempted, and overcome by small and trifling things.

He who is weak in spirit, and in some degree yet carnal, and prone to the things of time and sense, has considerable difficulty in dragging himself away from all earthly desires; and therefore he has often a feeling of sadness when he does withdraw himself from them, and is then easily provoked if any one thwarts him.

2. And, if he has followed his own desires, presently his conscience is burdened with a sense of guilt; because, by yielding to his passion, he has made no advance towards gaining that peace which he was in quest of.

True peace of mind, therefore, is got by resisting the passions, and not by allowing them to rule us.

There is no peace, then, in the heart of a carnal man, nor in the man who has given himself to the pursuit of outward things, but only in the spiritual and fervent.

CHAPTER VII.

Of avoiding vain Hope and Self-esteem.

1. HE is vain who puts his trust in man, or in created things.

Be not ashamed to serve others for the sake of our Lord Jesus Christ, and to be looked upon as poor in the eyes of the world.

Be not self-confident, but put your trust in God.

Do what you can, and God will co-operate with your good endeavours.

Do not trust in your own knowledge, nor in the skill of any living being; but rather in the Grace of God, Who helps the humble, and humbles the self-presuming.

2. If you possess riches, do not glory in them, nor in friends, because they are influential; but glory in God Who provides you with all things, and above all desires to give you Himself.

Be not proud of your height, or good looks, for a sickness may soon disfigure or deform you.

Do not take pleasure in thinking of your gifts or abilities, lest you displease God, from Whom we hold whatever good capacity we by nature possess.

3. You should not reckon yourself better than others, lest perhaps in the eyes of God, Who knows what is in man, you are considered worse.

Be not vain of your good works, because God's judgment is different oftentimes from man's; and what is pleasing to the one is displeasing to the Other.

If there is any good in yourself, believe that there is more in others, that you may preserve your humility.

It will not hurt you to put yourself under others; but it will be most hurtful to you to put yourself before others—even before one.

The lowly have continual peace, but the heart of the proud is continually disturbed by jealousy and indignation.

CHAPTER VIII.

That excessive Familiarity should be avoided.

1. "OPEN not thine heart to every man," but treat of your condition with one who is wise and fears God.

Be not often in the society of young people and strangers.

Do not seek to flatter the rich, nor to come into the presence of great men.

Associate with the humble and simple-minded, with the devout and well-behaved, and talk on edifying matters.

Be not familiar with any one woman, but in general commend all good women to God.

Love to hold intercourse with God alone and His angels, and avoid the acquaintance of men.

2. We must have charity towards all, but indiscriminate familiarity is not good. Sometimes it happens, that a person who is unknown to us has a bright reputation, whilst his presence at once causes him to sink in the opinion of those who are in his company.

We think to find favour with others when we

get on intimate terms with them; and the contrary is the result, for they are soon displeased by the faults they discover in us.

CHAPTER IX.

On Obedience and Subjection.

1. IT is a great advantage to live in obedience, and to be under the rule of another, and not to be one's own master.

It is far safer to be in subjection one's self than to be over others.

Many are under obedience rather from necessity than from choice; they regard it as a hardship, and murmur at the least thing. Neither do they gain freedom of mind, unless they entirely for the sake of God yield up their own will to Him.

Run hither and thither, you will find no rest save in humble subjection to the rule of one who is set over you.

A fancy for places and change have led many astray.

2. True is it, that each one likes to follow his own opinion, and has a preference for those who coincide with it. But, if God be with us, we ought to be willing to give up our own opinion for the blessing of peace.

Who is so wise that he can fully know all things?

Be careful, then, not to trust too much to your own judgment, but be willing to hear what others have to say.

If your opinion seem good, and yet you resign it for God's sake, and follow another, you will find that thereby you will make greater spiritual progress.

3. I have often heard it said, that it is safer to listen and take advice than to give it.

It is possible to happen, that each one's opinion may be good; yet to be unwilling to acquiesce in the sentiments of others, when there is just reason for doing so, is the mark of pride and obstinacy.

CHAPTER X.

Of Talking too much.

1. AVOID, as much as may be, busy throngs of people; for the transaction of worldly affairs is a great hindrance, even when they are entered upon with a sincere intention, for we are soon contaminated and ensnared by vanity. I oftentimes wish that I had kept silence, and had not been in company.

But why is it we so often speak and enter into conversation one with another, when, nevertheless we seldom relapse into silence without a wounded conscience?

The reason why we are so ready to talk is that we try to comfort each other by long conversations, and want to relieve our minds—wearied with various thoughts. And we very willingly speak and think of those things which we love or desire, or of the things which we regard as grievances.

2. But, alas, this is often in vain and to no purpose; for this outward consolation entails no small loss of that which is inward and divine.

Therefore we must watch and pray, lest the time pass away idly.

If it is right and proper for you to speak, say what will tend to edification.

A bad habit and carelessness about spiritual advancement are sure to lead to unguardedness of speech.

Yet to confer devoutly one with another on spiritual subjects is no small help towards progress in holiness, and this is especially the case, when persons of like mind and temperament are in religion associated together.

CHAPTER XI.

Of acquiring Peace, and of earnest desire for growth in Grace.

1. WE might have much peace, if we would not busy ourselves with the sayings and doings of others which are not our concern.

How can any one long remain in peace who meddles in other people's matters, and goes about in quest of causes of distraction, and is hardly ever quite recollected?

Blessed are the simple-minded, for they shall enjoy great peace.

2. Why were some of the Saints so perfect and contemplative? Because they endeavoured to mortify entirely all their earthly desires, and therefore could cling to God with their inmost hearts, and had time to attend to themselves.

We are too much occupied with our own passions, and too anxious about transitory things.

For seldom do we completely overcome a single fault, nor do we aim at daily improvement,—therefore we remain cold and lukewarm.

3. If we were quite strict with ourselves, and not entangled with outward things, then we should be able to taste the savour of Divine

things, and should have some experience of heavenly contemplation.

The chief impediment—and indeed the only one—is that we are not free from our passions and lusts, and do not strive to advance in the path of perfection, as the Saints have done.

When, then, any little trial comes, we are at once cast down, and take refuge in human consolation.

4. If, like brave men, we made an effort to stand in the battle, certainly we should find that the Lord helped us from Heaven.

For He Who arranges that we should have temptations, in order that we may put forth the effort to overcome them, will Himself be at hand to help those who are striving and trusting in His grace.

If we place our progress in religion only in outward observances, our spiritual life will soon come to an end.

The axe must be laid to the root of the tree, that—being freed from passions—we may possess peace of mind.

5. If we were to root out one bad habit every year, we should make considerable progress towards perfectness of life.

But, on the contrary, we often seem to feel that we were better and purer in the beginning of our conversion than we are now, after many years of profession.

Our fervour and profiting ought each day to increase, but now it is considered a great thing if any one is able to retain some portion of his first fervour.

If we were a little severe with ourselves at the beginning, we should afterwards be able to do all things with ease and delight.

6. It is hard to leave off that which we are accustomed to, and harder still to go against our own will.

But if you do not conquer little and easy things, when will you overcome those which are more difficult?

Resist at the very first your inclination, and give up bad habits, lest, perchance, you become more and more bound by them.

Oh, if you would but consider what peace you might procure for yourself, and what joy for others, by well-doing, I believe you would be more concerned about your spiritual progress.

CHAPTER XII.

Of the Profitableness of Adversity.

1. IT is good for us sometimes to have grievances and crosses; for they often make a man enter into himself, and remember that here he is in a state of banishment, and therefore must not set his hopes on things of the earth.

It is good for us sometimes to suffer contradiction, and to be badly or disparagingly thought of, even when we do and mean well.

These things often aid us in forming humility, and protect us from vain-glory; for then we love to turn to God as the inward witness, when we are defamed by the world and not thought well of.

2. Therefore a man should so thoroughly rest in God, as not to feel the need of many human consolations.

When a good man is afflicted, tried, or harassed with evil thoughts, then he discovers more his need of God, without Whom he perceives that he can do nothing.

He bemoans his state, and prays on account of the miseries he endures.

Then he is weary of living any longer, and wishes for death, that he might "depart and be with Christ."

Then, also, he is fully assured, that perfect security and full peace cannot be had in this world.

CHAPTER XIII.

Of Resisting Temptations.

1. AS long as we are in the world we shall always have tribulation and temptation. Therefore it is written in Job that man's life upon earth consists of temptation.

Therefore each one ought to be concerned about his temptations, "and watch unto prayer;" so that the Devil—who never sleeps, but "walketh about, seeking whom he may devour"—may not entrap him.

No one is so holy and perfect as not sometimes to be assaulted, nor can we be entirely exempt from temptations.

2. There are, moreover, temptations which are positively advantageous to us, though in themselves they may be troublesome and grievous; for by them a man is humbled, purified, and taught.

All the Saints passed through many tribulations and temptations, and derived profit from them.

And those who could not endure temptation became reprobates and fell away.

There is no vocation so holy, and no place so retired, as to be beyond the reach of temptation and adversity.

3. No man can be entirely free from temptations as long as he lives, because the source of temptation is in ourselves, by the inheritance of a corrupt nature.

When one temptation or trial goes, another comes; and we have always something to suffer, for we have fallen from a state of happiness.

Many try to escape from temptations, and fall the more grievously into them.

Flight is not our only weapon, but patient endurance and true humility, whereby we become stronger than all our enemies.

4. He who only avoids the outward occasion of falling, and does not uproot the inner tendency to evil, will make but poor progress; indeed, temptations will the sooner return to him, and with greater force than ever.

By degrees, and with patience and long-suffering, you will by the help of God overcome, better than by harshness and your own impetuosity.

Often take counsel in time of temptation, and never be harsh with one who is tempted, but console him as you would wish to be consoled yourself.

5. The beginning of all evil temptations is

inconstancy of mind and too little trust in God.

For as a ship without a rudder is driven hither and thither by the waves, so a man who is negligent and inconstant is tempted in manifold directions.

Fire proves iron, so temptation tries a just man.

We are often ignorant of the amount of power we possess, but temptation makes manifest to us what we are.

We must watch, then, most of all in the beginning of a temptation, for then more easily is the enemy overcome, when he has not been allowed for a moment to enter our hearts, but was repelled from our doors at the very first knock. Thus it has been said—

> "Resist at once; the physic comes too late
> When maladies have grown inveterate."

For at the first there comes to the mind simply a thought, then a strong imagination, after that the feeling of pleasure, then an evil motion, then consent, and so by degrees the malignant enemy gains full possession, because he was not resisted at the beginning.

The longer a man continues slack in resisting temptation, the weaker he daily becomes, and the stronger becomes his Adversary.

6. Some experience sore temptations at the commencement of their spiritual life, and some at the end; whilst some seem to suffer from life-long temptations.

Some, again, are but little tried according to the wisdom and justice of the appointment of God, Who considers every man's state and deserts, and ordains all things for the salvation of His elect.

7. Therefore, we ought not to despair when we are tempted, but pray more fervently to God, that He may deign to help us in all our tribulations, Who—in the words of St. Paul—has promised that He "will with the temptation also make a way to escape, that ye may be able to bear it."

Let us, therefore, humble our souls under the hand of God in every temptation and trial, for He will save and exalt those who are lowly in heart.

8. By temptations and trials a man's advancement is tested, and thereby his reward is increased, and his virtues are revealed to the edification of others.

It is no great thing for a man to be devout and fervent when he has nothing to try him; but if in the time of adversity he bears up patiently, then there is hope that he has made considerable progress in religion.

Some are preserved from great temptations,

and are often overcome by those which daily occur; so that, being thus humbled, they may never presume upon themselves in great matters, who in small things find themselves weak.

CHAPTER XIV.

Of avoiding Rash Judgment.

1. TURN your eyes upon yourself, and avoid passing judgment upon other men's doings.

In judging others a man labours to no purpose, very often errs, and easily falls into sin.

But to judge and examine himself is always a labour full of profit.

Our judgment is often regulated by our liking, for a right judgment is often corrupted through some private affection.

If in all we did we had a pure intention for the glory of God, we should not be so easily disturbed by the opposition of our feelings.

2. But often something lurks within, or also occurs from without, and in either case we are drawn aside.

Many secretly seek their own interest or pleasure in what they do, and are not aware of it.

They seem, also, to enjoy peace as long as things turn out according to their own will; but if they are thwarted, they are quickly disturbed and depressed.

From a diversity of tastes and opinions, it is by no means a rare occurrence for dissension to arise between friends and fellow-citizens, and between religious and devout persons.

3. An old habit is with difficulty given up, and no one is willingly led away from his own views.

If you rely more on your own reason and efforts than upon the subduing power of Jesus Christ, you will but slowly if ever become an enlightened man; for God wills that we should be perfectly subjected to Him, and that all our reason should be outvied by the ardour of our love.

CHAPTER XV.

Of Works none from Charity.

1. WE must never do evil for the sake of any thing, nor for the love of any person. But it may happen, that a good work for the benefit of one who stands in need should be left undone, or that a better should be substituted for it; for then a good work is not lost, but a better put in its place.

Without charity the outward work brings no

profit to the doer; but whatever is done out of charity—be it ever so small and contemptible—becomes fruitful, inasmuch as God takes more account of the dispositions of the doer than of the amount of his work.

2. He does much who loves much.

He does much who does what he has to do well.

He does well who serves the common good rather than his own will.

Many actions which are really carnal seem to spring from charity; for natural inclination, self-will, self-interest, or self-pleasing will seldom be absent.

3. He who has genuine and perfect charity, in nothing seeks himself, but desires God to be glorified in all things.

Also he envies no one, for he does not want to keep any joy for himself alone; neither does he wish to rejoice in himself, but above all good things to find his blessedness in God.

He attributes nothing that is good to man, but refers all things to God, from Whom all things proceed; in Whom, as in their end, all the Saints find their fruition and repose.

Oh, if one had a spark of true charity, how would all earthly things seem full of vanity!

CHAPTER XVI.

On Bearing with the Defects of Others.

1. WHATEVER a man cannot amend either in himself or in others he ought to bear patiently, until God orders things otherwise.

Consider that it may be advantageous that it should be so, for your trial and growth in patience, without which our merits are of little worth.

You ought, however, when you labour under such difficulties, to pray that God would vouchsafe to help you to bear them meekly.

2. If any one, after having been admonished once or twice, does not yield, do not contend with him, but commit all to God, that His Will may be done, and that He may be honoured by all His servants; for He knows well how to turn evil into good.

Strive to be patient in bearing the defects of others and their manifold infirmities; because you yourself have many also, and they have to put up with them.

If you are not yourself such as you would wish to be, how can you expect to find another according to your liking?

We would have others perfect, yet nevertheless we do not amend our own faults.

3. We would see others severely corrected, yet we do not wish to be corrected ourselves.

The great license given to others displeases us, yet we do not like to be denied anything ourselves.

We like others to be bound by strict rules, but we ourselves will in nowise endure restraint.

Thus it is evident, then, how rarely we weigh our neighbour in the same balance in which we weigh ourselves.

If all were perfect, what then should we have to suffer from others for the sake of God?

4. But now God has so ordained it, that we should learn to bear one another's burdens, for there is no one who has not some defect, no one without some burden, no one independent of others, no one wise enough of himself; but we ought to bear with one another, comfort one another, help, instruct, and advise one another.

The degree of virtue any one possesses is best manifested in times of adversity. Trials do not cause human frailty, but they serve to display what a man really is.

CHAPTER XVII.

Of a Life apart from the World.

1. YOU must learn to subdue self in many ways, if you would live in peace and concord with others.

It is no small thing to live in a religious community, or to be in close contact with many persons, and yet to converse without offence, and continue faithful even unto death.

Blessed is he who has thus lived holily and died happily.

If you wish, as you should, to stand firm and to progress in your spiritual life, regard yourself as an exile and stranger upon earth.

Men must become "fools for Christ's sake," if they would lead a religious life.

2. It was wisely said, "The tonsure does not make the monk," but a change of conduct, and a complete mortification of the passions, make a truly religious man.

He who does not seek in everything simply and purely the glory of God, and the salvation of his own soul, will find nothing but trouble and sorrow.

He also is not able to remain long in peace, who does not endeavour to take the lowest place and to be subject to all.

3. Remember that you are here to serve, not to rule; that you are called to suffer and work, not to waste your time nor to gossip.

Here, therefore, men are tried as gold in the furnace.

Here no one can abide, unless he is ready to humble himself with all his heart for the love of God.

CHAPTER XVIII.

Of the Examples of the Holy Fathers.

1. BEHOLD the bright examples of the holy Fathers, in whom true perfection beamed, and you will then see that all we do is little or nothing.

Alas, what is our life when it is compared with theirs!

The Saints and friends of Christ served their Lord in hunger and thirst, in cold and nakedness, in toil and weariness, in watchings and fastings, in prayers and holy meditations, in many persecutions and reproaches.

2. Oh, how many and how great were the tribulations through which Apostles, Martyrs, Confessors, Virgins, and all the rest, passed, who have willed to follow the footsteps of Christ! For they hated their lives in this world that they might keep them unto life eternal.

Oh, how strict and self-denying a life was that which the Holy Fathers led in the desert! how long and grievous were the temptations they endured! how often were they assaulted by the Enemy! what frequent and earnest prayers did they offer up to God! what rigid fasts they kept! what great zeal and fervour they had for their spiritual progress! what a brave war they carried on for the subdual of their vices! what a pure and single eye they had to the glory of God!

By day they worked, and by night they had time for long prayer; although, in the midst of their labours, they were far from letting go the spirit of prayer.

3. They passed all their time usefully; every hour seemed too short to spend with God. And through the great sweetness they enjoyed in prayer, sometimes they even forgot their bodily necessities.

They renounced all riches, dignities, honours, friends, and relations. They desired to possess nothing of this world.

Scarcely did they allow themselves the necessaries of life, and they grieved that they were at all under the necessity of ministering to the body.

They were poor, therefore, in earthly things, but rich indeed in grace and virtues.

They were outwardly in want, but within they

were replenished with grace and Divine consolation.

4. They were strangers to the world, but very near and intimate friends of God.

In their own eyes they seemed to be as nothing, and by the world they were despised, but in the eyes of God they were precious and beloved.

In true humility they stood firm, in simple obedience they lived, in charity and patience they walked; and, therefore, daily they progressed, and obtained great favour with God.

They were given for an example to all who are religious, and ought to have more power to provoke us to advance than many who are lukewarm have to influence us to relax.

5. Oh, how great was the fervour of all religious persons when Communities were first instituted!

How great their devotion in prayer! how great their longing for virtue! how vigorous their discipline! how reverence and obedience to those set over them were in high repute!

Their footprints—still remaining—testify that they were indeed holy and perfect men, who, by so valiant a struggle, trampled under foot the world.

Now he is reckoned to be great, who just escapes open sin or bears patiently his lot in life.

6. O lukewarmness and negligence concerning our state! that we so soon fall away from our first fervour, and grow weary of life through slothfulness and tepidity.

Would that the desire of spiritual growth was not wholly dormant in you who have had such opportunities of witnessing the lives of devout persons!

CHAPTER XIX.

On Religious Exercises.

1. THE life of a good religious person ought to be enriched with all virtues, so that his inner life might accord with his outward profession.

Indeed his inner life ought to be in advance of his outer; for God beholds the heart, and before all others we are bound to reverence Him wherever we may be, and—like the angels—to keep ourselves pure in His sight.

We ought every day to renew our resolutions, and to kindle our fervour, as though it were the very beginning of our conversion, and to say—"Assist me, O God, in this my good purpose, and in Thy Holy Service, and grant that this day I may begin perfectly, for that which I have hitherto been able to carry out is as nothing."

2. Our success depends upon the strength of our purpose; and, if we would make much progress we must use much diligence.

But, if one often fails after making a strong resolution, how will it fare with those who seldom make any good purpose, or who purpose without firmness?

But in various ways it comes to pass that we abandon our good purposes, and a slight omission in our devotions hardly ever happens without some loss to our souls.

The purposes of just men depend for their fulfilment rather upon the grace of God than upon their own wisdom; and, in whatever they take in hand, they always trust in His help.

For man proposes, but God disposes; for man's way is not in himself.

3. If from a call of duty, or for the benefit of another person, sometimes one of our regular devotions is omitted, it may be easily afterwards recovered again. But if, through distaste or negligence, it is readily given up, such conduct is sinful, and will be found to be hurtful to ourselves.

Strive as much as ever we can, we shall still be sure to fall short in many things.

Yet, always let us have something definite after which we are aiming; and let our resolves turn upon those things which we feel most of all hinder us.

We must examine and set in order both our outer and our inner life, because both are of importance to our spiritual advancement.

4. If you cannot continuously preserve recollection, at all events do so sometimes, and at least once a day;—for instance in the morning, or at evening.

In the morning make your resolution; in the evening examine yourself—your thoughts, words, and actions during the day, for in these, perhaps, you will find that you have oftentimes offended God and your neighbour.

Gird yourself like a man against the wicked devices of the Devil; curb your appetite, and you will more easily restrain the lusts of the flesh.

At no time be entirely idle, but either be reading, or writing, or praying, or meditating, or doing something for the common good.

Yet bodily mortification must be undertaken with discretion, and not equally by all.

5. Practices which are not general ought not to be paraded before others, for things which are singular are more safely carried out in secret.

You must, however, be careful not to neglect things which are performed by all, whilst you are eager for those which are only prescribed by yourself.

But having faithfully and fully performed the former, which are binding on you; if time remains, you may employ yourself in devotions according to your taste.

All cannot have the same plan of prayer, but one kind of devotion is suitable to one, another to another. Again, different devotions please us according to the different seasons; some delight the soul on Festivals, others on ordinary days; some we need in times of temptation, others in times of peace and quietness.

Some subjects we like to dwell upon when we are sad, others when we are rejoicing in the Lord.

6. About the time of the great Festivals we ought to renew our good practices of devotion, and ask more fervently for the prayers of the Saints.

From Festival to Festival we ought to make our resolve, as though we were then about to leave the world, and to pass at once to the Eternal Festival.

Therefore we should carefully prepare ourselves at such holy times, and pass them more devoutly, and keep more strictly all our observances, as though shortly we were about to receive the reward of our labours from God.

7. And if our departure should be delayed, let us think that we are not yet well enough

prepared, and that we are unworthy as yet of so great glory as that which shall be revealed in us at the fore-ordained time; and let us strive to become better prepared for death.

"Blessed is that servant," saith St. Luke, "whom the Lord when He cometh shall find watching. Verily, I say unto you, He will make him ruler over all He hath."

CHAPTER XX.

On the Love of Solitude and Silence.

1. SEEK a convenient time to devote to yourself, and meditate often on the benefits which God has bestowed on you.

Leave curious matters, and read such subjects as are calculated to produce compunction more than occupation of mind.

If you withdraw yourself from superfluous conversations and inquisitive restlessness, as also from hearkening to news and rumours, you will find that you have sufficient and fitting time for making good meditations.

The greatest Saints—whenever they were able to do so—shunned human companionship, and preferred to live in secret with God.

2. "Whenever I have associated with men," said one, "I returned from them less a man than

I was before." We have often experienced the truth of these words, when we have had a long conversation.

It is easier to be silent altogether than to speak with moderation.

It is easier to remain at home than to keep well on one's guard in society.

He, therefore, who aims at attaining to a more interior and spiritual life, must, with Jesus, depart from the crowd.

No one can with safety appear in public, unless he himself feels that he would willingly remain in retirement.

No one can with safety speak who would not rather be silent.

No one can with safety command who has not already learnt to obey.

No one can with safety rejoice, unless he has the testimony of a good conscience.

3. Yet, whatever feeling of security the Saints possessed, it was accompanied with a great fear of God. Nor could they be less anxious about themselves and humble, because they were conspicuous for their great virtues and grace.

But the security of the wicked arises from pride and presumption, and at the end is converted into despair.

Never promise yourself security in this life,

although you may be a good religious person or a devout hermit.

4. Oftentimes those who stand high in men's estimation are the more in danger on account of their too great self-confidence.

Therefore, for many it is better that they should not altogether be free from temptations, but be frequently assaulted, lest they should seem too secure, and perhaps be puffed up with pride; and, it may be, give themselves too much license as to worldly comforts.

Oh, how good a conscience would he preserve who never sought after fleeting joys, and who never entangled himself with the things of this world!

Oh, what great peace and repose would he possess, who would banish every vain anxiety, and think only upon profitable and Divine subjects, and place his whole trust in God.

5. No one is worthy of heavenly consolation, who has not sought diligently to deepen in himself the grace of compunction.

If you want to feel compunction, enter into your closet, and shut out the tumult of the world, as it is written,—"Commune with your own heart, and in your chamber, and be still."

You will find in your chamber what out-of-doors you too often lose.

If you keep up the habit of retiring for prayer,

you will find it sweet; but if it is irregularly done a distaste for it will be the result.

If in the commencement of your spiritual life you form the habit of retirement well, and keep it, afterwards it will become to you a dear friend and a most refreshing solace.

6. In silence and quiet the devout soul advances, and learns the hidden things of Scripture.

There the soul finds floods of tears, wherewith it nightly washes and cleanses itself, that it may become the more familiar with its Maker, the more remote from all the turmoil of the world its time is passed.

He, therefore, who withdraws himself from acquaintances and friends, to him will God with His holy angels draw near.

It is better to lead a hidden life, and to look well to the care of one's own soul, than to work miracles and neglect one's self.

It is praiseworthy in a man who has given himself to a Religious life, seldom to appear in public, to avoid being seen, and not to wish to see others.

7. Why do you wish to see that which it is not lawful for you to have? "The world passeth away, and the lust thereof."

The desires of sense lead us to roam abroad; but when the hour has passed, what do you bring back with you but a burdened conscience and a distracted mind?

A joyful departure often leads to a sad return, and a late and merry evening makes a sad morning.

So every carnal delight insinuates itself, but in the end it bites and destroys.

8. What do you see elsewhere, which you may not see here? Behold the heaven and the earth, and all the elements: for of these all things are made.

What can you see anywhere which can last long under the sun?

Perhaps you think that you will become satisfied, but you will never attain to that state.

If you saw the world and all that is in it in one view, what would it be but an empty vision?

Lift up your eyes to God on high, and pray Him to forgive your sins and negligences.

Leave vanities to the vain, but give your attention to those things which God has commanded you.

Close your door upon you, and call to you Jesus, your Beloved. Abide with Him in your closet, for you will not find such peace elsewhere.

If you had not gone forth, nor listened to idle reports, you would the better have continued to enjoy the blessing of peace. But in that you sometimes take pleasure in hearing news, it must follow that you will suffer perturbation of mind.

CHAPTER XXI.

Of Compunction of Heart.

1. IF you wish to make spiritual progress, keep yourself in the fear of God, and do not allow yourself too much liberty. Let your senses be all under control, and do not give yourself up to foolish mirth.

Give yourself to compunction of heart, and you shall find devotion; compunction leads the way to many blessings, which dissipation has the effect of quickly driving away.

It is wonderful that a man can ever be perfectly joyful in this life, when he considers and ponders upon his state of exile, and the many dangers to which his soul is exposed.

2. Through levity of mind, and thoughtlessness as to our defects, we become insensible to the sorrows of our soul, and so often vainly laugh when we really ought to weep.

There is no true liberty or real joy but in the fear of God with a good conscience.

Happy is the man who can put away every

OF COMPUNCTION OF HEART

distraction that hinders him, and can gather himself up again for communion with God in the spirit of compunction.

Happy is the man who renounces everything which may bring a stain or burden upon his conscience.

Strive manfully; habit is overcome by counter-habit.

If you are wise enough to leave other men to themselves, they will be sure to leave you alone to transact your own business.

3. Do not busy yourself in others' concerns, nor entangle yourself in the affairs of the great.

Keep your eye always upon yourself in the first place, and especially admonish yourself in preference to admonishing all your friends.

If you have not the favour of men, do not on that account be disheartened; but let it be a matter of grave concern to you, that you are not living so well and circumspectly as it becomes a servant of God and a devout religious person to live.

It is often better and safer for a man not to have many comforts in this life, especially bodily comforts.

The reason we have not Divine consolations, or but seldom find delight in prayer, is because we do not seek compunction of heart, and do not renounce all vain and outward sources of consolation.

4. Consider yourself unworthy of Divine consolation, and rather deserving to have much tribulation.

When a man has perfect compunction, the whole world becomes burdensome and bitter to him.

A good man finds sufficient cause for sorrow and for tears; for whether he regards himself, or thinks of his neighbour, he knows that no one lives here without tribulation; and the more strictly he examines himself, the greater ground for sorrow he discovers. The subjects for just sorrow and compunction of heart are our sins and evil inclinations, in which we lie so entangled as to be rarely able to contemplate heavenly things.

5. If you were more often to think upon your death than upon the length of your life, no doubt you would more earnestly try to amend.

If you were to weigh well in your mind the thought of Hell—the future torments of body or of soul, I believe you would willingly undergo sorrow and labour in this world, and not shrink back with fear from any austerity.

But because these things do not touch our hearts, and we still love the pleasures of this life, therefore it is we continue to be cold and very slothful in matters of religion.

It is often from lack of spirit that our miserable body is so quickly ready to complain.

Pray, therefore, humbly to the Lord, that He may give you the spirit of compunction; and say with the Prophet,—" Feed me, O Lord, with the bread of tears, and give me plenteousness of tears to drink."

CHAPTER XXII.

Of the State of Human Misery.

1. YOU are miserable wherever you are, and whatever way you turn yourself, unless you turn to God.

Why do you disturb yourself when things do not fall out according to your own wish and desire?

Who is there that has everything according to his own will?—neither I, nor you, nor any living man.

There is no one in the world without some trouble or distress, though he be king or pontiff.

Who is it who is best off? He indeed who is able to suffer something for God.

2. Many weak-minded and foolish people say, "Look how happy that man is! how rich and great he is! how powerful and exalted!"

But raise your eyes to heavenly riches, and

you will see that all these temporal things are nothing, and are very uncertain and often burdensome, for they are never possessed without anxiety and fear.

A man's happiness does not consist in abundance of temporal goods, but a moderate supply is sufficient for him. Indeed, it is a misery to live on the earth.

The more spiritual a man becomes, the more bitter is this present life to him, because he sees and understands more clearly the corruption of human nature.

For to have to eat and drink, to watch and sleep, to rest and labour, and to be subject to the other necessities of nature, is indeed a great misery and affliction to a devout man, who would fain be released and freed from all sin.

3. For the inward man is much weighed down by the necessities of the body in this life. Wherefore the Prophet devoutly prays that he may be delivered from them, saying—O Lord "bring thou me out of my distresses."

But woe unto those who do not know their own misery; and a greater woe to those who love this miserable and corruptible life!

For there are some who to such an extent cling to it, that—although by toil or begging they can only just get the necessaries of life—could they always live here below, they would care nothing for the Kingdom of God.

4. O how foolish and faithless in heart are those, who are so immersed in earthly things, that they have no relish but for that which is carnal.

But these miserable men will find out in the end to their great grief, how worthless and good for nothing was that upon which they had set their affections.

But the Saints of God and the devout friends of Christ did not care for the things which pleased the flesh, nor for the things which glittered but for a while; for, with all the hope and eagerness they possessed, they panted after eternal joys.

Their whole desire was borne upward towards that which abides and is invisible; lest, by the love of that which is visible, they should be drawn down to things below.

5. Be careful, brother, not to lose the hope of making progress in the spiritual life, for you have still time and opportunity.

Why do you wish to put off your good purpose? Arise, and begin at once, and say,— "Now is the time for action, now is the time for effort, now is the fit time for amendment."

When you are in trouble and affliction, then

will be the time for gaining the reward of patience.

You must pass "through fire and water," before you are brought out "into a wealthy place."

Unless you do violence to yourself, you will not get the victory over your corrupt nature.

As long as we carry about this frail body with us, so long shall we be unable to be without sin, or to live without weariness and pain.

We would gladly be at rest from all misery; but because we have lost innocence through sin, we have also lost true blessedness.

Therefore we must have patience, and wait for the mercy of God, "until this tyranny be over-past" and mortality is "swallowed up of life."

6. O how great is human frailty—always prone to evil!

To-day you confess your sins, and to-morrow you commit again the same faults you confessed.

Now you purpose to be on your guard, and in an hour's time you act as if you had made no purpose at all.

We have reason then to humble ourselves, and never to think highly of ourselves; because we are so weak and unstable.

That, also, which with much labour and difficulty we have by grace acquired, can quickly be lost through negligence.

7. What, then, will become of us in the end, who are so little in earnest in the morning of life!

Woe to us, if we so wish to turn aside to rest, as if it were already peace and safety, when there is not yet to be seen a vestige of true holiness in our conversation!

It would be a good thing, if—like young beginners—we could be taught anew the principles of a holy life; if, perchance, there might be hope of future amendment and of greater spiritual progress.

CHAPTER XXIII.

Of Meditation on Death.

1. VERY soon all will be over with you here; consider, then, your state before God.

To-day man is, and to-morrow he is gone.

But when he is taken out of sight, he quickly passes also out of mind.

Oh, the dulness and hardness of the human heart, which thinks only on the present, and does not rather provide for the things which are to come!

In every thought and act you ought so to hold yourself, as if you were going to die this very day.

If you had a good conscience, you would not much fear death.

It would be more to the purpose to shun sin than to flee from death.

If you are not prepared to-day, how will you be to-morrow?

To-morrow is an uncertain day, and how do you know that you will live till to-morrow?

2. What profit is it to us to live long, when we make such a poor use of our time?

Ah! a long life does not always bring with it amendment, but it often increases our guilt.

Would that we passed a single day in this world without fault!

Many reckon how many years it is since their conversion, yet often there is but small fruit of their amendment.

If it is fearful to die, perhaps to live long will be more dangerous.

Blessed is he who has always before his eyes the hour of death, and daily disposes himself for death.

If you have seen any one die, remember that you will pass through the same ordeal.

3. When it is morning, think that you may not see the evening; and when it is evening do not venture to make certain of reaching another morning.

Always then be ready, and so live that death may not find you unprepared.

Many die suddenly and unexpectedly—"For the Son of Man cometh at an hour when ye think not."

When that last hour shall have come, you will begin to feel very differently about all your past life, and to grieve greatly at your negligence and remissness.

4. O how happy and wise is he who now endeavours to become in life such as he would wish to be found at the hour of death.

Perfect contempt of the world, fervent desire of advancing in virtues, love of discipline, labour of penitence, readiness of obedience, denial of self, and endurance of any adversity for the love of Christ, will produce in us great confidence that we shall die happily.

When you are well you are able to do many good works, but I do not know what you can do when you are ill.

Few are made better and reformed by sickness; so those who are always moving from place to place seldom become holy.

5. Do not rely on friends and neighbours, nor put off the work of salvation to the future, for men will forget you sooner than you think.

It is better now seasonably to provide for the future, and to lay up in store a good foundation for the time to come, than to trust to the assistance of others.

If you are not solicitous about yourself now, who will be solicitous about you hereafter?

The present time is very precious; "now is the day of salvation," "now is the accepted time."

But, alas! that you should spend it so fruitlessly, when in it you might be gaining the treasure of everlasting life!

The time will come when you will desire one day or one hour in which to amend, and I know not whether it will be granted you.

6. Oh, dearest friend, from what peril may you deliver yourself, from what terror may you rescue yourself, by having at all times a due fear and anticipation of death!

Strive now so to live, that you may be able in the hour of death to rejoice rather than to fear.

Learn now to die to the world, that you may then begin to live with Christ.

Learn now to despise all things, that then you may be able to pass without regret to Christ.

Now keep under your body by mortification, that you may then have a full assurance.

7. Ah! fool, why do you imagine that you are going to live a long time, when you are not certain of a single day?

How many have been deceived in this respect, and unexpectedly snatched away!

How often have you heard such accounts as these,—such an one was slain; of another, that he was drowned, or had died from a fall; of another, that he died whilst at table, or at play!

One by fire, another by sword, a third by pestilence or violence comes to his end. Thus death is the end of all, and man's life passes away quickly like a shadow.

8. Who will remember you after you are dead, and who will pray for you?

Do, do now, dearest friend, whatever you can for yourself; because you do not know when you will die, nor what will happen to you afterwards.

Whilst you have time, amass for yourself incorruptible riches.

Think on nothing but on your salvation.

Care only for the things of God.

Make now to yourself friends, by venerating the Saints and by copying their actions, that when you fail in this life, they may receive you into everlasting habitations.

9. Keep yourself as a stranger and pilgrim upon the earth,—as one to whom the affairs of the world are no concern.

Keep your heart free, and lifted up to God, for here you have "no continuing city."

Direct thither day by day your sighs, your prayers, your tears, that your spirit after death may be worthy to pass with joy into the presence of the Lord. Amen.

CHAPTER XXIV.

On Judgment, and the Punishments of Sinners.

1. IN all things look to the end, and remember that you will have to stand before a strict Judge, from Whom nothing is hidden, Who is not to be bribed by gifts, and Who will admit no excuses, but will judge according to that which is right.

O most miserable and foolish one! what will you—who sometimes are afraid of the face of mere man when he is angry—then be able to answer unto God, Who knows all your evil-doings?

Why do you not make some provision for yourself against that Day of Judgment? Then no one can be excused or defended by another, but each one will bear his own burden, and it will be as much as he can do.

Now your labour is fruitful, your crying acceptable; now your groanings may be heard, and your sorrow atone for the past and have a cleansing effect.

2. The patient man has a great and salutary purgation, if, when injured, he grieves more for the malice of the other than for his own suffering; if he willingly prays for his enemies, and from his heart forgives their offences; if he is not slow to seek the pardon of those he might have offended; if he is sooner moved to compassion than to wrath; if he frequently does violence to himself, in order to bring the flesh into entire subjection to the spirit.

It is better now to purge out our sins, and to cut off our vices, than to reserve them to be purged hereafter.

Truly we practise deception upon ourselves through the inordinate love which we have for the flesh.

3. What else will that fire devour, unless it be your sins?

The more you spare yourself now, and gratify the flesh, the more severe will be the wrath you are treasuring up for yourself, for you are adding fuel to the fire.

In the things in which a man has sinned, in those will he be the more grievously punished.

There the slothful will be urged on with burning goads, and the glutton will be tormented with great hunger and thirst.

There the luxurious and the lovers of pleasures shall have showered upon them flaming pitch and stinking brimstone; and the envious, like mad dogs, shall howl from remorse.

4. There is no vice which shall not have its corresponding torment.

There the proud shall be filled with every kind of confusion, and the covetous shall be pinched with most wretched penury.

One hour of punishment there will be more bitter than a hundred years of the heaviest penance here!

There will be no cessation there, no interval of consolation to the damned.

Here occasionally there is rest from our labours, and the enjoyment of the consolation of friends.

Be now anxious about yourself, and grieve for your sins, that in the Day of Judgment you may with the Blessed be in safety.

For "then shall the righteous man stand in great boldness before the face of such as have afflicted him, and made no account of his labours."

Then shall he stand to judge, who now humbly submits himself to the judgments of men.

Then shall the poor and humble have great confidence; and the proud, on the other hand, shall fear on every side.

5. Then will it be seen that he was wise in

this world, who learnt for Christ to be considered a fool and to be despised.

Then every tribulation, patiently borne, will bring us joy, "and all iniquity shall stop her mouth."

Then shall every devout man rejoice, and the irreligious man shall mourn.

Then shall the flesh which was afflicted triumph more than if it had always been pampered with luxuries.

Then shall the shabby clothing become resplendent, and the fine garment be in the shade.

Then shall the poor cottage be more commended than the gilded palace.

Then shall persevering patience stand by us more than all the power of the world.

Then simple obedience shall be exalted more than all worldly astuteness.

6. Then shall a pure and simple conscience rejoice the heart more than all secular learning.

Then shall the contempt of riches weigh more than all the treasures of worldlings.

Then shall you receive more consolation from the prayers you earnestly said, than from having partaken of delicacies.

Then shall you rejoice at having kept silence, more than from the remembrance of long conversations.

Then shall works wrought by grace profit you more than many fair speeches.

Then shall a strict life and severe repentance be of more avail than all earthly delights.

Learn now to bear suffering a little, that you may be delivered from greater trials then.

Try here first what you may be able to bear hereafter.

If now you cannot bear so slight a suffering, how will you be able to bear eternal torments?

If now a little suffering makes you to such an extent impatient, what then will Hell do?

Remember, you can by no means have both joys—the joy of the world now, and the joy of reigning with Christ hereafter.

7. If hitherto you have always lived in honours and pleasures, what would it profit you if you were to die this very moment?

All things, therefore, are vanity, except to love God, and to serve Him only.

He who loves God with all his heart fears neither death, nor punishment, nor judgment, nor hell, because perfect love gives a safe access to God.

But he who still takes pleasure in sin fears death and judgment, and no wonder that he should do so.

Yet it is in a measure good, if love does not

yet recall you from evil, that at least fear of Hell should keep you from it.

But he who lays aside the fear of God cannot long remain in a good way, but will very soon fall into the snares of the Devil.

CHAPTER XXV.

Of Earnest Amendment of our Whole Life.

1. BE watchful and diligent in the service of God, and often reflect upon the nature of your calling and your promise to renounce the world. Was it not that you might live unto God, and become a spiritual man?

Therefore you should be eager to progress, for in a little while you will receive the reward of your labours. Then shall there be no more fear or sorrow in your borders.

Now you will labour a little, and you shall find great rest—yes, perpetual gladness.

If you continue faithful and fervent in your work, God will doubtless be faithful and bountiful in rewarding you.

You ought to preserve a good hope of attaining your crown, but it doth not behove you to feel secure, lest you should grow negligent or presumptuous.

2. When some one in suspense—who had often

wavered between fear and hope—on a certain occasion, being oppressed with grief, had prostrated himself in prayer before an altar, he said within himself—"O that I could know that I should persevere to the end!" and immediately he heard a voice within him reply: "And if you knew it what would you do? Do now what you would do then, and you shall be quite secure."

And being at once consoled and strengthened, he committed himself to the Divine Will, and his anxious disquietude ceased. He no longer wanted curiously to ask questions concerning his own future, but he rather sought to find out what was the acceptable and perfect will of God for the beginning and completing of every good work.

3. "Trust in the Lord, and do good," saith the prophet, "so shalt thou dwell in the land and be fed."

There is one thing which keeps many back from spiritual progress and earnest amendment of life, and that is, a horror of the difficulty and labour of the conflict.

Those mostly outstrip others in forming virtues, who strive to overcome those things which are most grievous and repugnant to themselves.

For the more a man conquers himself, and is mortified in spirit, so much the more does he progress in holiness, and the more grace does he acquire.

4. But all men have not equally much to overcome and mortify.

Yet he that is diligent and zealous will make greater progress, though he has more passions to subdue, than another who is good-natured, but less eager in the pursuit of virtues.

There are two things which greatly help forward our amendment, namely,—to withdraw ourselves forcibly from that particular evil towards which we have a vicious tendency, and earnestly to pursue that particular good of which we stand mostly in need.

You should make it a point to avoid and overcome in yourself those faults, which are most displeasing to you in others.

5. You will everywhere gain some spiritual profit, if, whatever good examples you may see or hear of, you are stirred up to imitate.

But if you see anything reprehensible, be careful not to copy it; and if you find that you have sometime committed the same fault, endeavour at once to correct yourself.

As your eye observes others, so others in turn observe you.

O how sweet and pleasant it is to see brethren earnest and devout, well-mannered and disciplined!

And how sad and grievous it is to see others walking disorderly, and not fulfilling the duties of their calling!

How mischievous it is to neglect the obligations of our state of life, and to turn our attention to things which are not our business!

6. Remember the resolution you have made, and set always before your eyes the Image of the Crucified.

You may well be ashamed, as you contemplate the Life of Jesus Christ, when you see how little you have endeavoured to make your own life like His,—long as you have walked in God's way.

A religious person, who earnestly and devoutly gives himself to the contemplation of the most holy Life and Passion of our Lord, will find in it in abundance all that is profitable and needful for him; nor will he require to seek out of Jesus for anything better.

Oh, if Jesus Crucified could enter into our hearts, how quickly should we learn all that is necessary!

7. An earnest religious person bears and takes all things well, which are enjoined upon him.

A religious person who has become slothful and lukewarm has trouble upon trouble, and suffers anguish on every side; because he lacks consolation from within, and may not seek it from without.

A religious person who ceases to live by discipline, exposes himself to some grave fall.

He who looks out for the more lax and easy way, will always be in distress; because something or another will be sure to chafe him.

How do so many other religious persons do, who live most strictly in retirement from the world, who rarely go out, who are withdrawn from external objects, who have very poor food, wear coarse clothing, do hard work, talk but little, keep long watches, rise early, spend much time in prayer, read often, and have always a strict guard over themselves?

Consider how in ancient times the Carthusians, the Benedictines, the Cistercians, and other religious orders, used to rise every night in order to sing psalms to God.

And therefore it would be shameful for you to be slothful, and never to take any pains in so holy a work, whilst so great a multitude of religious persons thus rejoice in God.

9. Oh, that we had nothing else to do but to praise our Lord God with all our heart and voice!

Oh, if you never required to eat, or drink, or sleep, but could always praise God and be occupied only in spiritual things, then you would be much more happy than you are now, when the necessities of the body demand your attention.

Would that there were no such necessities, but only the spiritual refreshments of the soul, which, alas, we seldom enough taste.

10. When a man comes to such a pitch of holiness as not to seek consolation from any created thing, then God begins to satisfy him entirely with His sweetness; and, after that, he is well contented to let things take their course.

He will not be carried away with joy in prosperity, nor unduly depressed in adversity, but will put his whole trust and confidence in God, Who is his all in all; in reference to Whom nothing fails or dies, for "all live unto Him," and unceasingly fulfil His Will.

11. Always remember the end, and that time lost never returns.

Without care and diligence you will never acquire virtues.

If you begin to grow lukewarm, you begin to be in a bad way.

But if you give yourself up to lead a fervent life, you will find great peace, and feel that your labour is lightened by the grace of God and by the love of virtue.

An earnest and diligent man is prepared for all things.

There is more toil in resisting our vices and passions than in hard manual labour.

The man who does not avoid small defects, will by little and little fall into greater.

You will always be glad in the evening, if you have spent the day profitably.

Watch over yourself, stir up yourself, caution yourself; and, whatever may be the case with others, neglect not yourself.

The more violence you do to yourself, the greater will be your growth in grace. *Amen.*

BOOK II.

CHAPTER I.

Of the Inner Life.

1. "THE kingdom of God is within you," saith the Lord.

Turn you with your whole heart unto the Lord, and forsake this miserable world, and your soul shall find rest.

Learn to despise outward things, and to give yourself to inward, and you shall feel the Kingdom of God arise within you.

For the Kingdom of God is joy and peace in the Holy Ghost; and this is not given to the wicked.

Christ will come to you and reveal to you His consolation, provided that you prepare for Him a worthy dwelling-place within you.

All His glory and beauty are from within, and there He delights Himself.

Many visits He makes to the inner man, and holds sweet colloquies with the soul, soothing it, filling it with peace, and admitting it to an exceedingly wonderful familiarity with Him.

2. O faithful soul! prepare your heart for this Spouse, that He may deign to visit you and abide within you.

For thus He says: "If any man love Me, he will keep My words, and We will come unto him, and will make Our abode with him."

Give Christ, then, a place in your heart, and refuse admission to all others.

When you possess Christ, you are rich, and have enough.

He will provide for you, and be faithful in supplying all your wants, so that you need not trust in man.

For men soon change, and quickly fail; but "Christ abideth for ever," and will stand by us firmly even unto the end.

3. There is no great reliance to be placed in a frail and mortal man, though he may be helpful and dear to us; neither should we be much grieved, if at times he should be against us and contradict us.

Those who are with you to-day may be against you to-morrow, and the opposite may be the case, for men often change like the wind.

Place your whole trust in the Lord, let Him alone be your fear and your love. He Himself will answer for you, and will do what is best for you.

Here you have "no continuing city," and wherever you are you are a stranger and a pilgrim; nor will you ever find rest, unless you are inwardly united to Christ.

4. Why do you fasten your eyes upon surrounding objects, when this is not the place of your rest? In Heaven ought to be your dwelling-place, and all else should be regarded as only that through which we have to pass.

All things pass away, and you pass away with them.

See that you do not cleave to them, lest you be ensnared by them and lost.

Let your thought be with the Most High, and your prayer without ceasing be directed to Christ.

If you are unable to meditate upon high and celestial subjects, rest in the contemplation of the Passion of Christ, and dwell with delight in His Sacred Wounds.

For if you fly devoutly to the wounds and glorious marks of Jesus, you will find great comfort in times of trouble, and will pay little account to the slights of men, and will easily bear all that slanderers may say against you.

5. Christ was also in this world despised by men, and in His extreme necessity was forsaken

both by friends and acquaintances, in the midst of reproaches.

Christ willed to suffer and to be despised, and do you dare at all to complain?

Christ had enemies and backbiters, and do you wish to have all men for friends and benefactors?

How would patience gain its crown, if you had no adversity in your lot?

If you want to suffer no contradiction, how can you be the companion of Christ?

Suffer with Christ, and for Christ, if you wish to reign with Christ.

6. If you had but once perfectly entered into the Heart of Jesus, and had tasted a little of His ardent love, then you would pay but little regard to your own convenience or inconvenience, but would rather rejoice when you had some opportunity offered you of bearing reproach, because the love of Jesus makes a man despise himself.

A lover of Jesus and of Truth—a truly spiritual man, and one free from inordinate affections—can freely turn himself to God, and can raise himself above himself in spirit, and rest in the enjoyment of God.

7. He who estimates all things according to their true value, and not according to their name or reputation, is indeed a wise man, and taught of God rather than of man.

He who knows what it is to live an inner life, and to count outward things of little importance, does not require special places, nor wait for set times to perform his devotions.

A spiritual man quickly gathers himself up, and never allows himself to be absorbed in outward things.

Outward occupation is no hindrance to him, nor the business which for the time may be necessary, but as things happen so he suits himself to them.

He who is inwardly well-disposed and disciplined, does not care for the strange and wayward behaviour of men.

A man is hindered and distracted, only when he draws things to himself.

8. If you were right in yourself, and your spirit well cleansed from sin, everything would tend to your profit and advancement.

Many things often displease you, and often disturb you; because you are not perfectly dead to yourself, neither are you detached from all earthly things.

Nothing to such an extent defiles and entangles the heart of man, as an impure attachment to creatures.

If you deny yourself external consolation, you will be able to contemplate heavenly things, and will often experience inward exultation.

CHAPTER II.

Of Humble Submission.

1. DO not make it a matter of moment, who may be for you or against you; but let it be your business and care, that God be with you in all you do.

Keep a good conscience, and God will well defend you.

The perversity of man cannot injure those whom God wills to befriend.

If you can suffer and be silent, you will doubtless experience the help of the Lord.

He knows the best time and manner of delivering you, and therefore you ought to resign yourself into His hands.

It belongs to God to help us, and to rescue us from all confusion.

The consciousness that others know our faults and reprove us, is often very helpful in preserving greater lowliness of spirit.

2. When a man is humbled because of his faults, he easily pacifies others, and quickly contents those who are offended with him.

God protects the humble and delivers him; He loves the humble and comforts him; He inclines His ear to the humble; He bestows great grace upon the humble, and after his humiliation He raises him to glory.

He reveals His secrets to the humble, and sweetly attracts and calls him to Himself.

A humble man, when he has to endure confusion of face, still remains fairly in peace; because he rests on God—not on the world.

You must not consider yourself to have made any advancement, unless you feel that you are inferior to every one else.

CHAPTER III.

Of a Good, Peaceful Man.

1. BE at peace, first, in yourself, and then you will be able to bring others into peace.

A peaceful man does more good than a learned man.

A passionate man even turns good into evil, and readily believes evil.

A good peaceful man turns everything to good.

He who is truly in peace never suspects others. But he who is ill at ease and discontented, is disturbed by various suspicions; neither does he rest himself, nor let others rest.

He often says what he ought not, and often

omits to do what he ought. He busies himself about what others ought to do, and neglects his own duty.

Let your zeal begin upon yourself, and then you may with justice extend it to your neighbours.

2. You know well enough how to excuse and palliate your own faults, but you are not willing to accept excuses for others.

It would be more just were you to accuse yourself, and excuse your brother.

If you wish to be borne with yourself, bear with others.

See what a distance you are as yet from that true charity and humility, which admit of indignation or anger with no one except with yourself.

It is no great thing to live peacefully with the good and gentle; for this is naturally pleasing to all, and every one likes to be at peace, and prefers those who agree with them.

But to be able to live in peace with those who are hard and obstinate, or who are undisciplined and contrary, is a great grace, and a highly praiseworthy and manly line of conduct.

3. There are some who are at peace in themselves, and live at peace with others.

And there are some who neither have peace in themselves, nor leave others in peace; these are a burden to others, and a greater burden still to themselves.

And others, again, there are who live in peace, and endeavour to bring others into the same condition.

And yet all our peace in this life is to consist in humbly bearing, not in escaping, the things we do not like.

He who knows best how to suffer aright, will be the one to enjoy the greater measure of peace. Such a man has gained the victory over himself, and is master of the world, and friend of Christ, and heir of Heaven.

CHAPTER IV.

Of a Pure Mind and a Simple Intention.

1. BY two wings a man is raised above the earth, namely, by Simplicity and Purity. Simplicity must be in the motive, purity in the affection; simplicity aims at God, purity embraces and tastes Him.

No good action will hinder you, if you are inwardly free from all self-seeking.

If you intend, and seek nothing else but to please God and benefit your neighbour, you will enjoy the feeling of inward liberty.

If your heart were right, then every creature

would be to you a mirror of life, and a book of holy teaching.

There is no creature so small and contemptible, as not to set before us something of the Goodness of God.

2. If you were inwardly good and pure, you would see all things without hindrance, and understand them well.

A pure heart penetrates Heaven and Hell.

Whatever a man's inward state is, his judgment on external matters will accord with it.

If there is such a thing as joy in the world, certainly the man who is pure in heart possesses it.

And if anywhere tribulation or distress are to be found, an evil conscience will experience it the most.

As iron when it is put into the fire, loses its rust, and becomes quite white with heat; so a man, when he is thoroughly converted to God, divests himself of his sluggishness, and is transformed into a new man.

3. When a man begins to grow cold, then he makes much of a little labour, and seeks outward consolation.

But when he begins to overcome himself without reserve, and to walk manfully in the way of God, then he thinks lightly of the difficulties which before were accounted insurmountable.

CHAPTER V.

Of the Consideration of One's Self.

1. WE cannot put much trust in ourselves, because we often stand in need of grace and wisdom.

. The light which is in us is but little, and we soon lose it by negligence.

We oftentimes, too, forget how great our inward blindness is.

We often do wrong; and, what is worse, excuse ourselves.

Sometimes, also, we are actuated by passion, and think it zeal.

We blame others for slight things, and overlook greater things in ourselves.

We are quickly enough sensitive about what we suffer from others, and dwell upon it; but what they have to bear from us, that we never think of.

He who well and rightly considers his own doings, is not likely to judge hardly concerning another.

2. A religious man puts the care of his own soul before all other concerns. And he who diligently attends to himself, is easily silent about others.

Never will you become spiritual and devout,

unless you are silent concerning others, and keep a special watch over yourself.

If you attend entirely to God and to yourself, external matters will but little affect you.

Where are you, when you are not with yourself?

And when you have run over all things, what advantage is it if you have neglected yourself?

If you would have peace, and true union with God, you must postpone all other considerations, and look only to your own spiritual life.

3. You will then make great progress, if you keep yourself free from all temporal anxiety.

You will fail greatly, if you set much value upon something temporal.

Let nothing be high, nothing great, nothing pleasing, nothing acceptable to you, except God Himself, or what is of God.

Regard the comfort which comes from the creature as altogether vain, whatever it may be.

The soul that loves God, despises all things that are less than God.

God Alone—the Eternal and Incomprehensible, Who fills all things—is the solace of the soul, and the true joy of the heart.

CHAPTER VI.

Of the Joy of a Good Conscience.

1. A GOOD man's glory is the testimony of a good conscience.

Keep a good conscience, and you will always be happy.

A good conscience can bear very much, and is able to be very cheerful even in adversity.

A bad conscience is always timid and uneasy.

You will enjoy a sweet peace, if your heart does not condemn you.

Never rejoice, unless you have done well.

The wicked never feel true joy, neither do they experience inward peace; for "there is no peace, saith the Lord, unto the wicked."

And if they say—"We are in peace, no evil will come to us; and who shall dare to hurt us?" believe them not; for suddenly the wrath of God shall arise, and their deeds shall be brought to nought, and their thoughts shall perish.

2. To glory in tribulation is no hard thing for him that loves, for thus to glory is to glory in the Cross of the Lord.

Short is the glory which is given by and received from men.

Sadness always follows the glory of the world.

The glory of the good is in their consciences, and not in the mouth of man.

The joy of the righteous is of God, and in God, and they rejoice in the Truth.

He who desires true and eternal glory, does not care for that which is temporal.

He who seeks earthly glory, or does not from his heart despise it, shews clearly that he has but little love for Heavenly.

He has great tranquillity of heart, who cares neither for praises nor reproaches.

3. He will be easily content and at rest, whose conscience is pure.

You are not more holy, because you are praised; neither are you more vile, because you are blamed.

For you are what you are, neither can you be made better by what others say than what God sees you to be.

If you take good heed to what in yourself you are inwardly, you will not care what men may say about you.

Man sees the face, but God sees the heart.

Man considers the actions; God weighs the motives.

To do well always and to think little of one's self, is the mark of a lowly spirit.

Not to wish for any consolation from any

creature, is a mark of great purity and inward confidence.

It is evident that the man who seeks no commendation from other men, has committed himself wholly to God.

"For not he that commendeth himself is approved"—saith blessed Paul—"but whom the Lord commendeth."

To walk inwardly with God, and to have the heart detached from earthly objects, is the state of a spiritual man.

CHAPTER VII.

Of Loving Jesus above All Things.

1. BLESSED is the man who knows what it is to love Jesus, and to despise himself for Jesus' sake.

We must leave what we love for the Beloved; for Jesus desires to be loved alone above all things.

The love of the creature is fallacious and fickle, the love of Jesus is faithful and enduring.

He who clings to the creature shall fall with the fallible, he who embraces Jesus shall stand firm in Him for ever.

Love Him, and keep Him for your friend, and He will stand by you when all other friends depart, and will not suffer you to perish at the last.

You must one day be severed from all, whether you will or not.

2. Keep near to Jesus both in life and in death, and commit yourself to His faithful care, Who, when all others fail, is able alone to help you.

Your Beloved is of such a nature, that He will not share your heart with another, but will have it all for Himself alone; and as a King will sit enthroned within it.

If you could be quite detached from all created things, Jesus would willingly make His abode with you.

Whatever, out of Jesus, you have reposed in man, you will find well-nigh lost.

Trust not nor lean upon a reed shaken with the wind; for all flesh is as grass, and all the glory of it shall wither as the flower of the field.

3. You will soon be deceived, if you regard only the outward appearance of man. For if you seek solace or gain from others, you will often experience loss.

If you seek Jesus in all, you will surely find Jesus.

But if you seek yourself, you will find yourself, and that to your own ruin.

For a man is a greater enemy to himself than

all the world, and than all his foes can ever be, if he does not seek Jesus.

CHAPTER VIII.
Of Familiar Friendship with Jesus.

1. WHEN Jesus is present all is well, and nothing seems difficult; but when Jesus is absent, everything becomes hard.

When Jesus does not speak to the soul, all other consolation is of no avail.

But if Jesus speaks only one word, there is a feeling of great comfort.

Did not Mary Magdalene instantly rise up from the place where she wept, when Martha said to her—"The Master is come, and calleth for thee"?

It is a happy hour, when Jesus calls you from tears to spiritual joy.

How dry and hard you feel without Jesus! How foolish and empty, when you seek anything out of Jesus! Is not this a greater loss, than if you lost the whole world?

2. What has the world to give you without Jesus?

To be without Jesus is a grievous Hell, and to be with Jesus is a delightful Paradise.

If Jesus is with you, no enemy can hurt you.

He who finds Jesus, finds a good treasure, yes, good beyond all good.

And he who loses Jesus, loses very much, ah! more than the whole world.

He is very poor who lives without Jesus; he is very rich, who has Him for his friend.

3. It is a great art to know how to hold converse with Jesus, and to know how to detain Him in the soul is great wisdom.

Be lowly and restful, and Jesus will be present with you.

Be devout and quiet, and Jesus will remain with you.

You may quickly drive Jesus away, and forfeit His grace, if you allow yourself to turn from Him to outward things.

And if you drive Him away and lose Him, to whom then will you fly, and whom then will you seek for a friend?

You cannot well live without a friend; and if Jesus is not your friend above all others, you will be very sad and desolate.

Therefore you act foolishly, if you lean upon or rejoice in any other.

You ought to prefer to have the whole world against you, rather than to offend Jesus.

Let Jesus be loved with a special love, beyond all who are dear to you.

4. Let all be loved for Jesus, but let Jesus be loved for Himself.

Jesus Christ alone is to be loved in preference to all, Who alone is found good and faithful above all friends.

For His sake, and in Him, both friends and foes must be dear to us; and we must pray for them all, that they all may know and love Him.

Do not desire to be to any one the sole object of praise or affection, for this is God's prerogative, Who has no one like unto Himself.

Never desire that any one in his heart should be taken up with the love of you, nor you with the love of any one; but let Jesus be in you, and in every good man.

5. Be pure and inwardly at liberty, and without undue attachment to any creature.

You must be stripped of all, and bring a pure heart to Jesus, if you would find rest, and see how sweet the Lord is.

And indeed this you will never attain to, unless you are prevented and constrained by His grace, so that, having forsaken and left all, you alone may be united to God alone.

For when the grace of God comes to a man, then he is able to do all things. And when it leaves him, then he becomes poor and weak, and seems reserved only for chastisement.

At such times you must not be cast down nor

give way to depression, but be conformed to the Will of God, and bear calmly whatever may come upon you for the glory of Jesus Christ; for after winter comes the summer, after night the day, after the storm the quiet calm.

CHAPTER IX.

Of the Absence of All Consolation.

1. IT is no great thing to despise human consolation, when you possess Divine.

It is a great, a very great thing, to be able to bear the absence of both human and Divine consolation; and for the love of God cheerfully to accept inward desolation, and never seek one's self, nor reflect upon one's deserts.

What great matter is it, if you are bright and devout when grace visits you? The hour of grace is to all a joyful one.

He rides with ease enough who is borne up by the grace of God.

And what wonder if he feels no burden, who is carried by the Omnipotent One, and led by the Sovereign Guide?

2. We like to have some consolation, and find it difficult to divest ourselves of self.

Saint Lawrence with the Prelate overcame the world, for all that seemed to bring pleasure in the world he despised; and Sixtus, God's High Priest, whom he exceedingly loved, he patiently suffered for the love of Christ even to be taken from him. Therefore he overcame the love of man by the love of the Creator, and chose rather to do God's good pleasure than to enjoy human comfort.

So you, too, learn to leave some relation or dear friend for the love of God.

And do not think it hard, when you are deserted by some friend, since you know that we must all one day be separated from one another.

3. A man must strive with himself much, and for a long time, before he can learn that he has fully overcome himself, and given his heart entirely to God.

When a man leans upon himself, he easily sinks back into human consolations.

But a true lover of Christ, and an earnest seeker after virtues, does not fall into those consolations, nor hunt for such sensible sweetnesses, but would rather undergo hard trials and endure toil for Christ's sake.

4. When, therefore, spiritual consolation is granted by God, receive it with thankfulness, and understand that it is from God's free gift, and not from your own merit.

Be not puffed up, nor overjoyed, nor vainly presumptuous, but rather be more humble on account of the gift, more cautious also and recollected in all your actions; since the hour of grace will pass away, and that of temptation will follow it.

When consolation is taken away, do not at once despair, but with humility and patience wait for a return of the heavenly visitation; for God is able to give you the next time a fuller consolation.

This is no new or strange experience to those who lead a spiritual life; for great Saints, and the Prophets of old, underwent oftentimes the same alternations.

5. Thus one says, when he was enjoying the presence of grace,—"In my prosperity I said, I shall never be moved."

But in the absence of grace, what he then experienced he afterwards describes thus,—"Thou didst hide Thy face from me, and I was troubled."

But then he by no means despairs, but more urgently prays to the Lord, and says,—"I cried to Thee, O Lord, and unto the Lord I made supplication."

At length, he relates the fruit of his prayer, and testifies that he had been heard, saying,—"The Lord hath heard me, and hath had mercy upon me; the Lord is become my Helper." But in what manner? "Thou hast turned for me my mourning into dancing," says he, "and girded me with gladness."

And if it has thus come to pass with great Saints, we—weak and poor creatures—ought not to be cast down, if at one time we are in coldness and at another time in fervour; for the Spirit comes and goes according to the good pleasure of His Will. Thus Job says—" Thou visitest him early in the morning, and suddenly Thou provest him."

6. Wherein then can I hope, or in what must I put my trust, save only in the great Mercy of God, and only in the hope of heavenly grace?

For whether I have with me good men, devout brethren, or faithful friends; whether I have with me holy books, beautiful treatises, or sweet chants and hymns, all bring me but little help or satisfaction, when grace forsakes me and leaves me in my own poverty.

At such a time no remedy is better than patience, and perfect self-surrender to the Will of God.

7. Never have I found any religious person who has not sometimes suffered from this withdrawal of grace, or has not experienced a decrease of fervour.

No Saint was ever so profoundly rapt or illuminated, as never to have known temptation from first to last.

For no one is worthy of the sublime contemplation of God, who for God has never endured tribulation.

For it is usual for tribulation to go before consolation, and to be a sign of its approach. For heavenly consolation is promised to those who endure temptation—"To him that overcometh," says He, "I will give to eat of the tree of life."

Divine consolation also is bestowed for the purpose of fortifying a man to bear adversity; and temptation follows to prevent spiritual pride.

The Devil is not asleep, and the flesh is not yet dead; therefore do not cease to prepare yourself for the conflict, for on your right hand and on your left are adversaries who never rest.

CHAPTER X.

Of Gratitude for the Grace of God.

1. WHY seek rest, when you are born to labour? dispose yourself for patience rather than comfort, for bearing the cross rather than for joy.

What worldly man is there who would not be glad to receive comfort and spiritual joy, if he could always get it? for spiritual consolations exceed all the delights of the world and pleasures of the flesh.

For all worldly delights are either infamous or vain; but spiritual delights alone are sweet and honest, are the product of virtues, and infused by God into pure minds.

But no one can always according to his own will enjoy these Divine consolations, because freedom from temptation does not long last.

2. A false liberty of mind and great self-confidence are much opposed to these heavenly visitations.

God does well in bestowing the grace of consolation, but man does ill by not at once giving all back with thanksgiving.

And on this account the gifts of grace cannot flow into us; because we are ungrateful to the Giver, and do not cause them all to flow back to their original source.

For grace is ever rightly his who gives or returns thanks; and from the proud shall be taken away that which is always given to the lowly.

3. I do not desire such a consolation as would remove the spirit of compunction from me; nor do I wish for such a power of prayer as would lead me into pride.

For not everything which is high is holy; nor everything that is sweet, good; nor every desire, pure; nor everything we love, dear to God.

I wish for the grace, which will make me more humble, and give me holy fear, and a greater willingness to renounce myself.

One who has experience both of the gift of devotion, and of the stroke which withdraws it, will not venture to attribute anything good to himself, but rather will confess that he is poor and naked.

Give to God what is God's, and attribute to yourself what is your own; that is, give to God thanks for His Grace, and perceive that you must ascribe to yourself only the fault, and the punishment which is due to the fault.

4. Put yourself always in the lowest place, and the highest shall be given you; for the highest does not stand without the lowest.

The highest saints before God are those who are least in their own eyes; and the more glorious they are, the more humble they become in themselves.

They can in no way be puffed up, because, being full of truth and heavenly glory, they are not desirous of vain-glory, but are grounded and established in God.

And those who, whatever good they have received, ascribe it to God, do not seek glory one of another, but seek that which comes from God alone; and they desire above all things that God should be glorified in Himself, and in all His Saints; and they ever act with this aim in view.

5. Be, then, thankful for that which is least, and you shall be worthy of greater gifts.

Let the least blessing be to you as a very great one, and a contemptible gift as one of special value.

If the dignity of the Giver be considered, no gift will appear small or inconsiderable; for that cannot be small, which is given by the most High God.

Yes, if He gives penalties and stripes, we ought to be grateful; for whatever is permitted to come to us, is ordered by Him for our salvation.

He who desires to retain the grace of God, should be grateful for the grace which God has given; should be patient when it is withdrawn; should pray that it may be restored; should be watchful and humble, lest it should be lost.

CHAPTER XI.

Of the Small Number of the Lovers of the Cross.

1. JESUS has now many lovers of His Heavenly Kingdom, but few bearers of His Cross.

He has many desirous of His consolation, but few of His tribulation.

He finds plenty of companions of His table, but few of His abstinence.

All wish to rejoice with Christ, but few wish to bear anything for His sake.

Many follow Jesus as far as the breaking of bread, but few to the drinking of the cup of His Passion.

Many reverence His miracles, but few follow the ignominy of His Cross.

Many love Jesus as long as things go well with them.

Many praise and bless Him as long as they receive certain consolations from Him.

But if Jesus were to hide His face from them, or forsake them for a little while, then they would begin to murmur, or grow depressed.

2. But those who love Jesus for the sake of Jesus, and not for some comfort of their own, love and bless him in every tribulation and anguish of heart, as well as in the highest consolation.

And if He never gave them comfort at all, they would still praise Him, and even give Him thanks.

3. O how powerful is the pure love of Jesus, when it is not mixed with any self-interest or self-love!

Are not those to be called hirelings, who are always seeking consolation?

Are not those manifestly lovers of themselves rather than of Jesus, who always keep in view their own advantage or gain?

Where is he to be found, who is willing to render to God a disinterested service?

4. Rarely is one found so spiritual as to be stripped of all things.

For where is the man to be found who is truly poor in spirit, and quite detached from all created things? "His value is (as of things brought) from afar, and from the ends of the earth."

If a man should give all he is possessed of, it is as yet nothing.

And if he should practise great penance, it is as yet little.

And if he should attain to all knowledge, he is yet afar off.

And if he has great virtue, and very ardent devotion, there is still much lacking to him.

"One thing is needful," and of the highest importance to him.

What is it? It is, that, having forsaken all things, he should forsake himself too; that he should entirely divest himself of self, and deny himself without reserve.

And when he has done all things which it was his duty to have done, let him think that he has done nothing.

5. Let him not think that great, which might be esteemed great; but let him in truth pronounce himself an unprofitable servant, as the Truth says,—"When you shall have done all things that are commanded you, say, We are unprofitable servants."

Then may he be poor and naked in spirit, when he can say with the Prophet, "I am all alone and poor."

Yet none richer, none more free, none more powerful than the man who knows how to forsake himself and all things, and to take the lowest place.

CHAPTER XII.

Of the Royal Way of the Holy Cross.

1. THIS seems a hard saying to many, "Deny yourself, take up your cross, and follow Jesus."

But it will be much harder to hear that last sentence, "Depart from Me, ye cursed, into everlasting fire."

For those who now willingly hear the preaching of the Cross, and practise what they hear, shall not then be terrified by the sentence of eternal damnation.

This sign of the Cross shall be in the heavens, when the Lord comes to Judgment.

Then shall all the servants of the Cross, whose lives have been conformed to the image of the Crucified, approach Christ, their Judge, with great confidence.

2. Why then are you afraid to take up the cross, when it will bring you to the Kingdom?

In the Cross is salvation, in the Cross is life, in the Cross is protection from our enemies, in the Cross is infusion of celestial sweetness, in the Cross is strength of mind, in the Cross is joy of spirit, in the Cross the height of virtue, in the Cross the perfection of sanctity.

There is no salvation for the soul, nor hope of eternal life, but in the Cross.

Take up, therefore, the cross, and follow Jesus, and you shall go into life everlasting.

He has gone before you, bearing His Cross, and has died upon the Cross for you, that you might also bear your cross, and be ready to die upon the cross.

Because, if you die with Him, you shall also live with Him; and if you have fellowship with Him in suffering, you shall also have fellowship with Him in glory.

3. Behold everything is in the Cross, and everything depends upon our dying on it; and there is no other way to life, and to true inward peace, save the way of the Holy Cross, and of daily mortification.

Go where you will, seek what you will, and you will find no higher way above, nor safer below, than the way of the Holy Cross.

Arrange and order all things according to your will and pleasure, and yet you will be certain to find something which you must suffer, either willingly or unwillingly, and so you shall find the cross always.

For either you will feel pain in the body, or in the soul you will sustain tribulation of spirit.

4. Sometimes you will be forsaken by God, sometimes tried by your neighbour; and—what is worse—often be a trial to yourself.

Neither can you be delivered nor eased by any remedy or solace, but you must suffer as long as God wills.

For God wills that you should learn to bear tribulation without consolation, and that you should submit yourself entirely to Him, and become more humble on account of the trial.

No one is so touched with a heartfelt sense of the Passion of Christ, as the man whose lot it has been to suffer like things.

The cross, then, is always at hand, and everywhere awaits you.

You cannot escape it, run where you will; for wherever you go, you take yourself with you, and you will always find yourself.

Look above you, look below you, look without

and within you, and everywhere you will find the cross; and it is necessary that you exercise patience everywhere, if you would preserve inward peace, and gain an everlasting crown.

5. If gladly you carry the cross, it will bear you and bring you to the longed-for goal, where there shall be no more pain,—although here that shall never be.

If you bear it unwillingly, you will make it burdensome, and increase its pressure, yet notwithstanding you will have to bear it.

If you cast away one cross, you will doubtless find another, and perhaps a heavier one.

6. Do you believe that you can avoid that which no mortal ever could escape? What Saint was ever in the world without the cross and trial?

For neither was our Lord Jesus Christ one hour without the sorrow of His Passion, as long as He lived.

"Christ," saith He, "must needs suffer, and rise again from the dead, and so enter into His Glory." And how can you seek any other way than this royal one—the way of the Holy Cross?

7. The whole life of Christ was a cross and a martyrdom, and do you seek after rest and pleasure?

You err, you err, if you seek anything else but to suffer tribulation; because the whole of this mortal life is full of miseries, and signed on all sides with crosses.

And the higher a person has advanced in the spiritual life, so much the heavier he will often feel his crosses become, for the pain of exile is intensified by love.

8. Yet, however, this man in his manifold afflictions is not without some consolation, for he is relieved by the thought of the very great fruits which result to him from bearing his cross.

For whilst he willingly submits himself to it, every burden of trial is turned into an assurance of Divine consolation.

For as the flesh is brought low by tribulation, in the same degree the spirit is strengthened by inward consolation.

And sometimes from an eager acceptance of trial and adversity on account of a desire to be conformed to the Cross of Christ, he derives so much strength, that he does not wish to be without sorrow and tribulation; since he has the conviction, that the more hard and grievous the things are he is capable of enduring for God's sake, the more acceptable he becomes in the sight of God.

It is not man's strength, but the grace of Christ which can fortify, and act in, the frail flesh; so that the things which would be always naturally abhorred and shunned, should through fervour of spirit be sought after and loved.

9. It is not in accordance with man's nature to bear the cross, to love the cross, to chastise the body and bring it into subjection, to flee honours, gladly to bear reproach, to despise himself, to wish to be despised by others, to bear all adversities with losses, and to desire no worldly prosperity.

If you look to yourself, you will find that none of these things you can do in your own strength.

But if you trust in the Lord, strength from above shall be given you, and the world and the flesh shall be made subject to you.

Neither shall you fear your enemy, the devil, if you are armed with faith, and signed with the Cross of Christ.

10. Set yourself, then, as a faithful and good servant of Christ, to bear manfully the Cross of your Lord, Who out of His love was crucified for you.

Prepare yourself to have many adversities, and much unpleasantness in this miserable life; for so it will be with you everywhere, and so you will be sure to find it, wherever you hide yourself.

So it must be, and there is no remedy by way of escape from tribulation and sorrow, but only patient endurance.

Drink lovingly of the Lord's cup, if you desire to be His friend, and to have part with Him.

Leave comforts to God's disposal; He will do what is best in reference to them.

But you—set yourself to bear tribulations, and regard them as the greatest consolations; for the sufferings of this present time are not worthy to deserve the glory which shall hereafter be revealed in us, even if one could bear them all.

11. When you have arrived at such a point as to feel trial to be sweet to you, and to relish it for Christ's sake, then think that it is well with you, for you have found a paradise upon earth.

As long as suffering seems grievous to you, and you seek to avoid it, so long will it be ill with you, and the anxiety to escape tribulation will continually attend you.

12. If you set yourself to what you ought, namely, to suffer and to die, it will soon become better with you, and you shall find peace.

Even if you should have been caught up to the third heaven with Paul, you would not on that account be secured from suffering any evil.

"I," said Jesus, "will shew him how great things he must suffer for My Name's sake."

Therefore to suffer awaits you, if you are pleased to love Jesus, and constantly to serve Him.

13. Would that you were worthy to suffer something for the Name of Jesus! How great glory would be laid up for you! how great exultation to all the Saints of God! how great edification to your neighbour!

For all recommend patience, although few wish to suffer.

Rightly you ought to suffer a little for Christ, when many suffer heavier trials for the sake of the world.

14. Know assuredly that you must lead a dying life; and the more any one dies to himself, so much the more does he begin to live unto God.

No one is fit to comprehend heavenly things, unless he has shewn himself ready to bear adversities for Christ's sake.

Nothing is more acceptable to God, nothing more salutary for yourself in this world, than that you should cheerfully suffer for Christ.

And if you have a choice in the matter, you ought to desire to suffer adversities for Christ, in preference to being refreshed with many consolations; for by the former you would be made more like unto Christ, and would have a closer resemblance to all the Saints.

For our merit and progress in our state of life are not reckoned by the number of our sweetnesses and consolations, but by patient endurance of many hardships and trials.

15. If, indeed, there had been anything better and more profitable for the salvation of mankind than suffering, Christ would certainly have shewn it by word and example.

For both the disciples who followed Him, and all who desire to follow Him, He openly exhorts to bear the cross, saying—"If any man will come after Me, let him deny himself, and take up his cross, and follow Me."

Therefore, when we have read through, and searched into all, let this be our final conclusion—"That through much tribulation we must enter into the Kingdom of God."

BOOK III.

CHAPTER I.

Of Christ's speaking inwardly to the Faithful Soul.

1. I WILL hearken what the Lord God will speak in me.

Blessed is the soul which hears within the Lord speaking, and receives from His mouth the Word of consolation.

Blessed are the ears which catch the breathings of the Divine whisper, and pay no heed to the whispers of the world.

Blessed indeed are the ears which listen not for the voice which sounds from without, but to the inner voice of truth.

Blessed are the eyes which are closed to outward objects, but intent upon inward.

Blessed are they who dive into things internal, and strive day by day through spiritual exercises to gain a deeper capacity for receiving heavenly secrets.

Blessed are they who are glad to devote their time to God, and break away from all worldly hindrances.

2. Consider these things, O my soul, and shut the doors of your senses, that you may be able to hear what the Lord God speaks within you.

Thus your Beloved says—"I am your salvation, your peace, your life;" "keep yourself with Me, and you shall find peace."

Dismiss all transitory things, and seek things eternal.

What are all temporal things but seductive, and what would be the good of all creatures, if you were forsaken by the Creator?

Bid farewell then to all things, and become a well-pleasing and faithful servant of your Creator, so that you may be able to lay hold of true blessedness.

CHAPTER II.

That Truth speaks inwardly without the sound of Words.

1. "SPEAK, Lord, for Thy servant heareth." "I am Thy servant: give me understanding that I may know Thy testimonies." Incline my heart to the words of Thy mouth, let Thy speech drop as the dew.

The children of Israel of old said to Moses, "Speak thou unto us, and we will hear: let not the Lord speak unto us, lest we die."

Not so, O Lord, not so, I pray you, but rather with Samuel, the prophet, I humbly and earnestly entreat, "Speak, Lord, for Thy servant heareth."

Let not Moses speak to me, nor any of the prophets, but rather do Thou, O Lord God,—Inspirer and Enlightener of all the prophets,—speak unto me; for Thou alone without them art able perfectly to instruct me, but they without Thee are of no avail at all.

2. They can indeed sound forth words, but cannot convey the spirit.

They speak most beautifully, yet, if Thou art silent, their words do not reach the heart.

They deliver the words, but Thou openest the understanding.

They bring forth mysteries, but Thou unfoldest the sense of what is signified.

They proclaim precepts, but Thou helpest us to keep them.

They shew the way, but Thou strengthenest us to walk in it.

They act upon us only outwardly, but Thou teachest and enlightenest the heart.

They water the surface, but Thou vouchsafest the increase.

They cry aloud with words, but Thou givest understanding to the hearers.

Let not Moses, then, speak to me, but Thou O Lord, my God, Eternal Truth, lest, if I only hear with the outward ear, and am not inwardly enkindled, I die and become unfruitful; lest the Word, heard but not acted on, known but not loved, believed but not kept, be turned to my condemnation.

Therefore "speak, Lord, for Thy servant heareth;" for "Thou hast the words of eternal life."

Speak to me, that it may be for some comfort to my soul, and for the amendment of my whole life, and also for Thy eternal praise and glory and honour.

CHAPTER III.

That the Words of God are to be heard with humility, and that many do not ponder them.

1. MY son, hear My words; My words are most sweet, surpassing all the knowledge of the philosophers and wise men of the world.

My words are spirit and life, and are not to be weighed by man's understanding. Neither are they to draw us to a vain complacency, but to be heard in silence, and to be received with all lowliness and with all affection.

And I said, 'Blessed is the man whom Thou chastenest, O Lord, and teachest him out of Thy law: that Thou mayest give him rest from the days of adversity, and that he may not be desolate in the earth.'

2. I—saith the Lord—have taught the prophets from the beginning, and even now I do not cease to speak to all; but many have hardened their hearts, and are deaf to My voice.

Many would rather listen to the world than to God; and more readily follow the desires of the flesh than the Will of God.

The world promises things temporal and small, and is served with great avidity: I promise things very great and eternal, and men render Me a heartless service.

Who is there that serves and obeys Me in all things with the same care as that with which the world and human masters are served?

'Be ashamed, O Zidon, says the sea,' and if you ask the cause, hear why:—" For a small reward men run a long way; for eternal life, many will scarce once lift their foot from the ground."

That which is valueless is sought after, for one coin sometimes there is a disgraceful litigation; for a trifling thing and a slight promise men shrink not from fatigue day and night.

3. But, alas! for a changeless good, for an inestimable reward, for the highest honour, and

eternal glory, they soon grow weary even with a very little labour.

Blush, therefore, O slothful and complaining servant, that those are found more ready to labour for death than you for life.

They rejoice more in vanity than you do in the truth.

Sometimes, indeed, they fail to realize their hopes; but My promise never fails, nor sends him empty away who trusts in Me.

What I have promised, I will grant; what I have said, I will fulfil; if only a man abides in My love—faithful to the end.

I am the Rewarder of all who are good, and the Mighty Prover of all who are devout.

4. Write My words on your heart, and meditate diligently upon them, for they will be found to be very needful in time of temptation.

What you cannot understand when you read, you shall know in the day of visitation.

In two ways I am in the habit of visiting My elect, namely, by temptation and by consolation; and daily I read to them two lessons, the one by rebuking their vices, the other by stimulating them to advance in virtues.

He that hears My words and despises them, has One Who shall judge him at the Last Day!

A Prayer

To implore the grace of Devotion.

5. O Lord my God, Thou art my only good; and who am I that I should dare to speak to Thee?

I am Thy most poor servant, and a vile and contemptible worm, poorer and meaner than I am aware of or dare to express.

Yet remember, O Lord, that I am nothing, and can do nothing, and possess nothing.

Thou only art Good, Just, and Holy; Thou canst do all things; Thou providest all things; Thou fillest all things, leaving only the sinner empty.

Call to mind Thy mercies, O Lord, and fill my heart with Thy grace, Thou Who willest not that Thy works should be void.

6. How can I bear this wretched life, unless Thy grace and Thy mercy sustain me?

Hide not Thy face from me; delay not to visit me; withdraw not Thy consolation, lest my soul become as parched land before Thee?

Teach me, O Lord, to do Thy Will. Teach me to walk humbly and worthily before Thee; for Thou art my wisdom, Thou knowest me as I am, Thou knewest me before the world was, and before I was born into it.

CHAPTER IV.

That we ought to walk before God in Truth and Lowliness.

SON, walk before Me in truth, and ever seek Me with simplicity of heart.

He who walks before Me in truth shall be preserved from evil assaults, and the truth shall deliver him from deceivers, and from the slanders of the wicked.

If the truth shall have made you free, you shall be free indeed, and shall take no account of the vain sayings of men.

O Lord, Thy word is true, may it ever be with me!

May Thy truth teach me, may it guard me, and keep me safe unto the end; let it free me from all bad and inordinate affections, and then I shall walk before Thee in great liberty of heart.

2. I will teach you (saith the Truth) what is right and pleasing in My sight.

Think over your sins with great regret and sorrow, and never allow any thought of self-esteem on account of good works.

In truth you are a sinner; you are subject to and entangled with many passions.

Of yourself you tend to nothingness, you

quickly fall, you quickly are overcome, you quickly lose peace, and quickly vanish away.

You have nothing then to boast yourself of, but have many grounds for counting yourself vile, for you are much weaker than you are capable of comprehending.

3. Therefore do not esteem any thing great of all you do.

Let nothing appear great, nothing precious and wonderful, nothing worthy of esteem, nothing high, nothing truly to be praised or desired, but that which is eternal.

Let Eternal Truth please you above all things, and your own exceeding vileness above all things displease you.

Fear nothing so much, find fault with and flee nothing so much, as your own vices and sins, which ought to be more displeasing to you than all worldly losses.

Some do not walk in sincerity before Me, but through curiosity and conceit are allured by the wish to know secret things, and to understand the deep things of God, to the neglect of the knowledge of themselves, and of their own salvation.

Such persons often fall into great temptations and sins, on account of their pride and curiosity, for I resist them.

4. Fear the judgments of God, tremble at the wrath of the Almighty One.

But do not discuss the works of the Most High, but examine your own iniquities, in how many ways you have offended, and how many good works you have neglected.

The devotions of some consist only in their books, of others in their pictures, of others in outward signs and gestures.

Some have Me on their lips, yet seldom in their hearts.

There are others who, being enlightened in their understanding and purified in heart, ever pant after eternal things, are weary if earthly things are spoken of, and regret that they have to attend to the requirements of nature; and these perceive what the Spirit of Truth speaks within them.

For He teaches them to despise earthly things, and to love Heavenly things; to disregard the world, and continually, day and night, to desire Heaven.

CHAPTER V.

Of the wonderful Effect of Divine Love.

I BLESS Thee, Heavenly Father, Father of my Lord Jesus Christ, because Thou hast deigned to be mindful of me, poor as I am.

O Father of mercies, and God of all comfort,

I give thanks unto Thee, Who sometimes refreshest me with Thy consolation, me—unworthy of any consolation.

I bless Thee and glorify Thee evermore, with Thy Only-begotten Son, and the Holy Ghost, the Comforter, for ever and ever.

Ah, Lord God, my Holy Lover, when Thou enterest my heart, my whole inward being shall rejoice.

Thou art my Glory and the Joy of my heart: Thou art my Hope and my Refuge in the day of my trouble.

2. But because my love as yet is weak, and my virtue imperfect, therefore I need to be strengthened and consoled by Thee.

Therefore visit me more often, and instruct me by Thy holy discipline.

Deliver me from evil passions, and heal my heart of all undue affections, so that being inwardly healed and thoroughly purged from sin, I may be made fit to love, brave to suffer, firm to persevere.

3. Love is a great thing, on all sides a great good; it alone can make the heavy burden light, and bears with evenness all inequalities. For it bears a burden without a sense of its weight, and makes every bitter thing sweet and pleasant.

The noble love of Jesus urges us to undertake

great things, and excites the desire to become more and more perfect.

Love wishes to tend upwards, and not to be held back by things beneath.

Love wills to be free, and detached from all worldly affection, that its inner sight may not be over-clouded; that it may not be entangled by any temporal interest, nor overthrown by any loss.

Nothing is sweeter than love, nothing stronger, nothing higher, nothing broader, nothing more pleasant, nothing better either in Heaven or earth, because love is born of God; and rising above all created things, can find its rest in Him alone.

4. One who loves, flies, runs, rejoices, and is free and unrestrained.

Love gives all for all, and has all in all, for it rests in Him Who is Sovereign and above all, and from Whom every good flows and proceeds.

Love looks not at the gift, but has its eye upon the Giver more than upon all goods.

Love often knows no limits, but is fervent beyond all bounds.

Love never feels a burden, never thinks things tasks, willingly attempts what is above its strength, never argues that things are impossible; because all things seem to it possible and lawful to be undertaken.

It seems able to do all things, and it does effect much, and takes in hand that which he who loves not would faint under and lie down.

Love watches, and slumbering does not sleep; if weary, it wearies not; if restrained, it is not straitened; if fearful, it is not dismayed; but as a living flame and glowing torch it bursts upward, and under all circumstances securely keeps its ground.

5. If any man loves, he will know what is the utterance of love.

A great cry in the ears of God is the ardent affection of the soul which says, "God, my God, my Love, Thou art wholly mine, and I am wholly Thine!"

6. Expand Thou my soul with love, that I may learn with the inward palate of my heart to taste how sweet it is to love, and to be dissolved in, and to overflow with love.

Let me be possessed by love—rising above myself through excessive fervour and rapture.

Let me sing the song of love, let me follow Thee my Beloved on high, let my soul exhaust itself in Thy praise; being jubilant through love.

Let me love Thee more than myself, and love myself only for Thee, and all others in Thee according to the law of love, which shines out from Thy Example.

7. Love is swift, sincere, tender, pleasant and sweet, courageous, patient, faithful, wise, long-suffering, noble, and never self-seeking; for whenever any one seeks his own advantage, he then falls from love.

Love is circumspect, humble, and upright; not yielding to softness, levity, or vanity; love is sober, steady, chaste, quiet, and keeps a guard over all the senses.

Love is subject and obedient to those in authority; to itself it seems worthless and contemptible; to God is devout and thankful—trusting and ever hoping in Him; even when God withdraws the sweetness of His Presence, for there is no life of love which is without sorrow.

8. He who is not prepared to suffer all things, and to give himself up to the will of the Beloved, is not worthy of the name of a lover.

A lover ought cheerfully to accept whatever is hard and distasteful for the sake of the Beloved, and not to falter in his affection, when all things seem to go against him.

CHAPTER VI.

Of the Test of a true Lover.

1. SON, you are not yet a valiant and wise lover.

Why, O Lord?

Because at a little opposition you give over what you have begun, and are too greedy for consolation.

A brave lover stands firm in the hour of trial, and does not listen to the cunning suggestions of the Enemy.

As he is pleased with Me in prosperity, so he is not displeased with Me in adversity.

2. A wise lover does not regard so much the gift of the lover as the love of the giver. He looks at his affection more than the value, and sets all gifts below him whom he loves.

A noble lover does not rest in the gift, but in Me above all gifts.

Therefore all is not lost, if sometimes you cannot feel as you would towards Me or My Saints.

That good and sweet affection, which sometimes you are sensible of, is an effect of present grace, and a sort of foretaste of the Heavenly Country, upon which you must not too much rely, for it comes and goes.

But to resist the evil thoughts which arise

within you, and to spurn the suggestions of the Devil, is a real sign of virtue, and of great merit.

3. Let not, then, strange imaginations disturb you, on whatever subject they may be presented before you.

Keep firmly your resolution, and your intention right towards God.

It is not an illusion, that you should be sometimes suddenly rapt in ecstasy, and then immediately after that your heart as usual should turn to mere trifles.

For such things come of themselves, and you suffer them unwillingly, and as long as they are displeasing to you and you resist them, so long is it a gain to you and not a loss.

4. Be aware that the old Enemy strives by all means in his power to hinder your desire for good, and to deter you from all religious exercises, namely, from the veneration of the Saints, from the devout remembrance of My Passion, from the profitable recollection of past sin, from a watchful spirit, from the firm purpose of advancing in virtue.

He suggests many evil thoughts, that he may weary you, and draw you away from prayer and from reading good books, and give you a dread of it.

He dislikes the lowly confession of your sins,

and would, if he could, keep you away from Holy Communion.

Do not believe him, nor pay regard to him, although he often draws near with subtlety to deceive you.

When he suggests bad and unholy thoughts, know from whom they come; say to him, "Begone, unclean spirit! be ashamed, wretched being! thou art abominable to whisper such things in my ears."

"Depart from me, most vile seducer! You shall have no part in me; but Jesus will stand by me, as a mighty defender, and you shall stand ashamed."

"I would rather die, and undergo any penalty than consent to your suggestions."

"Be silent, and hold your peace, I will not heed you any longer, however much you may molest me."

'The Lord is my light and my salvation, whom then shall I fear?'

'Though an host of men rose against me, yet should not my heart be afraid. The Lord is my Helper and my Redeemer.'

5. Fight like a good soldier; and if sometimes through frailty you fall, gather up anew your strength with more energy than before, trusting to a greater measure of My grace, and carefully avoiding all self-complacency and pride. Many

by this are drawn into error, and sometimes fall into a blindness almost incurable.

Let the fall of the proud and of those who are foolishly presumptuous be a warning to you, and lead you to cultivate an abiding lowliness of spirit.

CHAPTER VII.

Of hiding Grace under the guard of Humility.

1. MY son, it is better for you, and the safer course, to hide the grace of devotion, and not to be high-minded nor to speak much about it, nor think much about it; but rather to despise yourself, and to fear it, as given to one unworthy of it.

You must not cleave too tenaciously to this devotional feeling, for very soon you may experience quite the reverse.

When you have the feeling, think with yourself how miserable and poor you are when deprived of it.

Nor does spiritual advancement depend so much on the presence of devotional feelings as it does on bearing their withdrawal with humility, self-sacrifice, and patience; provided that you do not neglect your prayers, nor allow yourself to omit any other accustomed duty, but to the best of your power and ability do cheerfully what you can; and do not entirely neglect yourself because you feel spiritual dryness and disquietude.

2. For there are many who, if they do not at once succeed, grow impatient or slothful.

For the way of man is not always in his own power, but it is the part of God to give and console, when He wills, and as much as He wills, and to whom He wills, and as it pleases Him, and no more.

Some imprudent persons through devotional yearnings have overthrown themselves by wishing to do more than they could; not taking into account their own weakness, they follow their feelings rather than the judgment of their reason.

And because they presumptuously enter upon greater matters than God wills, they therefore quickly lose His grace; they become poor, and fall back into their own nothingness, who had built their nests on high; in order that, humbled and destitute, they may learn not to fly with their own wings, but to trust under the shadow of Mine.

Those who are fresh and inexperienced in the way of the Lord, unless they suffer themselves to be ruled by discreet persons, will easily fall into error, and be made a laughing-stock.

3. And if they will follow their own judgment rather than trust themselves to the experience of

others, their end will be most disastrous, if in spite of all remonstrance they still persist in their own course.

Those who are wise in their own conceits will seldom humbly submit to be ruled by others.

It is better to possess but little knowledge, and to be lowly and have poor capacities, than to have great treasures of learning, and vainly to think much of yourself.

It is better to have little than much, for of much you may be proud.

He does not act with sufficient discretion who gives himself entirely and without restraint to joy; forgetting his own previous indigence, and that chaste fear of the Lord, which is apprehensive of losing the grace which has been given.

Neither does he possess true moral wisdom, who in time of adversity or of any difficulty gives way to despair, and in his mind and feelings suffers the confidence which he should have in Me to lessen.

4. He who in time of peace would be too secure, will often be found in time of war to be too much cast down and fearful.

If you knew how always to continue humble and little in your own eyes, and how to rule and keep your spirit within due bounds, you would not fall so often as you do into danger and sin.

·It is a good plan when you are meditating, and the fire of devotion within you is kindled, to anticipate the time when it may be taken away.

And when this shall come to pass, remember that the light can return again, which, for your safety and for My Glory, I have for a while withdrawn.

5. Such a trial is often more profitable to you, than if you always had the prosperity which you wish for.

For a man's worth is not to be estimated by the number of visions and consolations which may be granted to him, nor by his knowledge of the Scriptures, nor by his high rank; but his moral greatness is to be ascertained by the depth of his humility, and the abundance of divine charity which he possesses, by the pure and single intention to the glory of God which is at the root of his actions, by his knowledge of his own nothingness, by a sincere contempt of himself, and by his joy being greater when he is despised by others and set aside than when he is honoured.

CHAPTER VIII.

Of a low estimation of one's self in the sight of God.

1. SHALL I speak unto my Lord, when I am but dust and ashes? If I regard myself as anything more, behold Thou standest against me, and my iniquities bear witness to the truth, and I cannot contradict it.

But if I count myself vile, and bring myself to my nothingness, and do away with all my self-esteem; and if I should sink down even to the dust (that which I am), then will Thy grace be in mercy granted to me, and Thy light be near my heart; and all self-esteem, even the least, shall be swallowed up in the valley of my nothingness, and perish for ever.

There Thou wilt show me to myself, what I am, what I was, and whence I came; for I am nothing, and I knew it not.

If I am left to myself, behold, I am nothing, and I am all weakness; but if Thou suddenly dost look upon me, at once I am made strong, and am filled with fresh joy.

And it is very wonderful, that I am so suddenly lifted up, and so graciously embraced by Thee, I—who by my own weight am always sinking to the bottom.

2. Thy undeserved love preventing me is the cause of it, succouring me in so many trials, guarding me also from grave dangers, and rescuing me from evils (for I may truly call them so) numberless.

For indeed by a false love for myself I lost myself; and by seeking Thee alone, and by a pure love for Thee, I have found both myself and Thee, and from that love have gained a deeper consciousness of my own nothingness.

Because Thou, O sweetest Lord, hast dealt with me above all desert, and beyond all that I dare hope for or ask.

3. Blessed be Thou, my God, for though I am unworthy of all Thy benefits, yet Thy Excellence and Infinite Goodness never cease to do good even to the unthankful, and to those who are turned away far from Thee.

Turn us to Thee, that we may be thankful, humble, and devout; for Thou art our salvation, our strength, and our defence.

CHAPTER IX.

That all things are to be referred to God, as to their Last End.

1. MY son, I ought to be thy highest, and thy last end, if you desire to be truly blessed.

By this intention shall your affections be purified, which are too often wrongly bent towards yourself and towards created things.

For if you have a selfish end in any thing, you will at once inwardly fail and become dry.

Therefore you should refer all things principally to Me, for I am He Who gave you all.

Regard each separate blessing, as flowing from the Supreme Good; and therefore to Me, as to their source, all things must be referred.

2. From Me, small and great, poor and rich, as from a living fountain, draw living water; and those who render Me a free and willing service shall receive grace for grace.

But he who desires to glory out of Me, or to delight in some private good, shall not be established in true joy, nor be enlarged in his heart, but shall meet with many hindrances, and be much straitened.

Therefore you must not ascribe any thing good to yourself, nor attribute anything that is good in any man to himself, but refer all to God, without Whom man has nothing.

I have given all, and I will to have all returned to Me again ; and with great strictness I require acts of thanksgiving.

3. This is a truth which puts vain-glory to flight.

And if Heavenly grace and true charity have entered the heart, there will be no envy, nor narrowness, neither will self-love take possession of it.

For Divine charity conquers all things, and expands all the powers of the soul.

If you are truly wise, you will rejoice in Me alone, you will hope in Me alone ; for there is none good but God alone, Who is to be praised above all, and to be blessed in all.

CHAPTER X.

That to serve God, when you have despised the World, is sweet.

1. NOW I will speak again, O Lord, and will not be silent; I will say in the ears of my God, and of my King Who is on high,—"O how great is the abundance of Thy Goodness, O Lord, which Thou hast laid up for them that fear Thee."

But what art Thou to those who love Thee?

what to those who serve Thee with all their heart?

Truly unspeakable is the sweetness of contemplating Thee, which Thou dost bestow on them that love Thee.

By this, most of all, hast Thou shewed me the sweetness of Thy love, that when I was not, Thou didst make me; that when I had wandered far from Thee, Thou didst bring me back again, that I might serve Thee; and didst command me to love Thee.

2. O Spring of Love unceasing, what shall I say of Thee?

How can I forget Thee Who hast condescended to remember me, even after that I was laid waste and had perished?

Thou hast dealt with me mercifully beyond all expectation, and hast manifested grace and friendship beyond all desert.

What shall I render unto Thee for this grace? For it is not given to all to forsake all, to leave the world, and retire into the Religious Life.

Is it any thing great that I should serve Thee, Whom every creature is bound to serve?

It ought not to appear a great thing to me, but this should seem great and marvellous to me, that Thou shouldest deign to receive one so poor and unworthy as I am into Thy service, and to make him one with Thy beloved servants.

3. Behold, all things are Thine which I have, and with which I serve Thee, and yet (strange contrast!) Thou servest me, rather than I Thee.

Behold, Heaven and earth, which Thou hast made for the service of man, are ready and waiting daily to do Thy Will whatsoever it may be.

And this is little: for even Angels Thou hast made and appointed for the service of man.

But that which surpasses all is, that Thou Thyself hast deigned to serve man, and hast promised to give Thyself to him.

4. What shall I give Thee for these thousands of benefits?

Would that I could serve Thee all the days of my life! Would that even for one day I could render Thee a worthy service! Truly Thou art worthy of all service, all honour, and of eternal praise.

Truly Thou art my Lord, and I am Thy poor servant, who am bound to serve Thee with all my strength, nor should I ever be weary of praising Thee.

This I wish, this I desire, and whatever is wanting to me do Thou deign to supply.

5. It is great honour and great glory to serve Thee, and to despise all things for Thy sake.

For they shall have great grace who freely take upon themselves Thy most holy service; and they shall find the sweetest consolation from the

Holy Ghost, who for Thy love have cast away all the pleasures of the flesh.

They shall experience great freedom of mind, who for Thy Name enter on the narrow way, and disregard all worldly anxieties.

6. O pleasant and delightful service of God, which makes a man in truth free and holy!

O sacred state of Religious service, which makes a man equal to Angels, pleasing to God, terrible to devils, and worthy to be commended by all the faithful!

O service to be embraced and ever desired, which will gain the Supreme Good, and secure the joy which shall last for ever!

CHAPTER XI.

That the Desires of the Heart are to be examined and restrained.

1. SON, you have many things which you must yet learn, and which as yet you do not properly know.

What are these, O Lord?

That you mould your desires entirely according to My good pleasure; and that you cease to love yourself, and that you become a jealous and eager lover of My Will.

Desires oftentimes inflame you, and make you

impetuous; but consider whether you are moved more on account of My honour or advantage, or for your own.

If you seek My interest, you will be quite contented whatever may be the result I ordain; but, if there is some latent seeking of self, lo, this brings hindrance and vexation.

2. Beware, therefore, that you lean not too readily upon some preconceived desire without having sought My counsel; lest, perhaps, afterwards you repent of it, and begin to regret the course you have adopted, which at first pleased you, and for which you were zealous, as it seemed the best.

For not every feeling which appears good is at once to be followed, nor should every opposite desire at the first be quenched.

Even in good endeavours and desires it is necessary sometimes to employ restraint, lest through eagerness you incur distraction of mind; lest through an undisciplined manner you become a scandal to others; or again, lest by the opposition of others you suddenly are disturbed and fall.

3. Sometimes indeed you must use violence, and manfully fight against sensual desires, not regarding what the flesh likes or does not like; but making it rather your business to bring the unwilling flesh into subjection to the spirit.

And so long ought it to be chastised and compelled to remain in subjection, until it is ready to accept all things, and to learn to be content with a little, and to be pleased with what is plain and simple, and never to grumble at any inconvenience.

CHAPTER XII.

Of cultivating Patience, and of striving against Lusts.

1. O LORD God, patience is very necessary, as I perceive, for there is much that goes contrary to us in this life.

For however much I may labour for peace, my life cannot be without sorrow and warfare.

It is so, My son, I do not will that you should seek a peace which is not interrupted by temptations, and which suffers no disturbance; but think, that then you have found peace, when you are tried by various troubles, and proved by manifold adversities.

2. If you say that you cannot endure much suffering, how will you bear the fires of another world?

Of two evils the less must always be chosen. Therefore that you may escape eternal torments hereafter, strive to bear present evils patiently for the sake of God.

Do you think that men of the world suffer nothing or little? You would not find it to be so, even if you asked those who lived most luxuriously.

But you will say, "They have many pleasures, and they do what they like, and therefore their troubles sit lightly upon them."

Be it so, that they have what they desire, but how long, do you think, it will last?

3. Behold, those who prosper in the world, as the smoke consume away, and retain no remembrance of their past joys.

But, even whilst they are alive, they do not rest in them without bitterness, and weariness, and fear.

For the self-same thing which brings them pleasure, frequently also brings with it the penalty of sorrow.

And it is just that it should be so, that having inordinately sought and followed after pleasures, they should not cram themselves with them without bitterness and shame.

4. O how short, how false, how inordinate and base, are all their pleasures!

Nevertheless so inebriated and blind are they that they have no understanding, but like dumb animals, for the sake of some passing delight of this corruptible life, they incur the death of the soul.

Thou, therefore, My son, "go not after thy lusts, but refrain thyself from thine appetites." "Delight thyself in the Lord, and He shall give thee the desires of thine heart."

5. For if you desire true delight, and to be plenteously comforted by Me, behold in the contempt of all worldly things, and in the cutting off of every vile gratification, shall be your blessing, and abundant consolation shall be rendered to you.

And the more you withdraw yourself from the consolations of creatures, so much the sweeter and more powerful shall be the consolations which you shall find in Me.

But at first you shall not attain to these consolations without some sadness and laborious struggle.

Ingrained habits will make resistance, but they can be overcome by the formation of better habits.

The flesh will complain, but by fervour of spirit it can be curbed.

The Old Serpent will urge you on, and harass you, but by prayer you can put him to flight; and beside that, by useful occupation you can in great measure prevent his approach.

CHAPTER XIII.

Of the obedience of humble subjection after the Example of Jesus Christ.

1. MY son, he who strives to withdraw himself from obedience, withdraws himself from grace; and he who seeks to enjoy things alone, forfeits the advantages which are in common.

If a man does not readily and willingly submit to his superior, it is a sign that his flesh is not yet in complete subjection, but often rebels and complains.

Learn, therefore, promptly to submit to the one who is over you, if you desire to bring your own flesh into subjection.

For more quickly is the external adversary vanquished, when the inner man has not been laid waste.

There is no more troublesome, no worse enemy of the soul, than you yourself are to yourself, when you do not follow the guidance of the Spirit.

It behoves you to conceive a true contempt of yourself, if you desire to prevail against flesh and blood.

2. Because you still love yourself too inordinately, therefore you shrink from resigning yourself entirely to the will of others.

But what great matter is it for you, who are but dust and nothing, to submit yourself to man for God's sake; when I, the Almighty and Most High, Who created all things out of nothing, have humbly subjected Myself to man for your sake?

I became the lowest and the last of all, that you may conquer your pride through My humility.

"Dust, learn to obey; dust and clay, learn to humble yourself, and bend down beneath the feet of all.

Learn to break down self-will, and to be ready to obey all."

3. Be fierce against yourself, and do not permit pride to remain in you; but exhibit such a humble and childlike demeanour, that all may be able to walk over you, and tread upon you as the dust of the streets.

What have you, vain man, to complain of? What, vile sinner, can you answer those who reproach you, you—who so often have offended God, and so often have deserved hell?

But Mine eye spared you, because your soul was precious in My sight; that you might know My love, and ever be thankful for My benefits; also, that you might give yourself continually to true subjection and humility, and bear patiently to be yourself despised.

CHAPTER XIV.

Of the consideration of God's Secret Judgments, in order that we may not be puffed up by any thing good in us.

1. THOU thunderest Thy judgments upon me, O Lord, and shakest all my bones with fear and trembling, and my soul is greatly terrified.

I stand astonished, and reflect—"that the heavens are not pure in Thy sight."

If in the Angels Thou hast found folly, and didst not spare them, what shall become of me?

Stars fell from heaven, and do I—but dust—dare to presume?

They, whose works seemed to deserve praise, have fallen to the lowest depths; and those, who used to eat the bread of Angels, I have seen delighting themselves with the husks of the swine.

2. There is then no sanctity, if Thou, O Lord, withdraw Thy hand.

No wisdom is of avail, if Thou cease to direct.

No courage helps, if Thou do not continue to defend.

No chastity is secure, if Thou do not protect it.

No watchfulness of our own avails, if Thou keep not Thy holy guard over us.

For when we are forsaken by Thee, we sink and perish; but when we are visited by Thee, we are raised up and live.

Indeed of ourselves we are unstable, but through Thee we are strengthened; of ourselves we grow cold, but by Thee we are enkindled.

3. O how humbly and how basely should I think of myself! how should I esteem as nothing whatever good I may seem to have!

O how profoundly ought I to submit myself to Thine unsearchable judgments, O Lord; when I find myself to be only nothing, even nothing!

O weight, not to be measured! O sea, not to be crossed, where I discover nothing about myself, save that I am simply nothing!

Where then is there a hiding-place for one vainglorious thought? where can be trust in my own strength?

All vainglory is swallowed up in the depths of Thy judgments towards me.

4. What is all flesh in Thy sight? Shall the clay boast itself against him that fashioned it?

How can he be puffed up by vain words whose heart is in truth subjected to God?

Not all the world could lift him up, whom the Truth had subjected to itself; neither shall he be moved by the praise of a multitude of men, who has firmly set all his hope in God.

For they also who praise him, behold they

are all nothing, and shall pass away with the sound of their words; but "the truth of the Lord endureth for ever."

CHAPTER XV.

What we ought to do or say with regard to everything we desire.

1. MY son, say in everything—"Lord, if it is pleasing to Thee, so let it be done.

"Lord, if it be for Thy Glory, let this be done in Thy Name.

"Lord, if it seem expedient to Thee, and receives Thy approbation, then grant me this that I may employ it to Thy Glory.

"But if Thou knowest that it will be hurtful to me, and not profitable to the salvation of my soul, take away from me this desire which I have."

For not every desire is from the Holy Ghost, though it may seem to a man a just, honest, and good desire.

It is difficult to judge aright about this or that desire, and to say whether it arises from a good or evil spirit; or, whether it is the prompting of your own heart.

Many have been deceived at last, who at first fancied they were led by a good spirit.

2. Therefore whatever desire may arise in the mind, it must always be desired and sought after with the fear of God, and with lowliness of heart; and above all, with self-resignation, you must commit the whole matter to Me, and say;—" O Lord, Thou knowest what is best for me, this or that; as Thou wilt, give me what Thou wilt, and as much as Thou wilt, and when Thou wilt.

"Deal with me as Thou knowest to be best, and as pleases Thee most, and to the furtherance of Thy glory.

"Place me where Thou wilt, and be free to dispose of me in any way.

"I am in Thy hand; turn me hither and thither through my course.

"Behold I am Thy servant, ready for all things, since I desire not to live for myself, but for Thee, and would that I could do so worthily and perfectly!"

A Prayer

That the Good Will of God may be fulfilled.

3. Grant me, O most merciful Jesus, Thy grace, that it may be with me, and labour with me, and abide with me even to the end.

Give me grace ever to desire and to will what is most acceptable to Thee, and most pleasing in Thy sight.

Let Thy Will be mine, and let my will ever follow Thine, and fully accord with it.

Let there be between Thee and me but one will, so that I may love what Thou lovest, and abhor what Thou hatest; and let me not be able to will anything which Thou dost not will, nor to dislike anything which Thou dost will.

4. Grant that I may die to all things which are on the earth, and for Thy sake love to be despised, and to be unknown in the world.

Grant to me—above all things to be desired—that I may rest in Thee, and that my heart may find its peace in Thee.

Thou art the peace of my heart, Thou, its sole repose; out of Thee all things are hard and unquiet.

In this very peace, that is, in Thyself, the Sole, the Supreme, the Eternal Good, I will sleep and take my rest. Amen.

CHAPTER XVI.

That true comfort must be sought in God Alone.

1. WHATEVER I can desire or imagine for my comfort, I do not look for it here, but hereafter.

For if I could have all the comforts of this

world, and enjoy all its delights, it is certain that they could not last long.

Wherefore you cannot, O my soul, be fully comforted, nor perfectly refreshed except in God, Who is the Comforter of the poor and the Defender of the humble.

Wait a little, O my soul, wait for the Divine promise, and you shall have abundance of all good things in Heaven.

If you unduly desire the things which are present, you will lose those which are eternal and heavenly.

Use the temporal: desire the eternal.

You cannot satisfy yourself with any temporal goods, because you were not created for the purpose of enjoying them.

2. Though you had all created goods, you could not be happy and blessed; but in God, Who made all things, your whole blessedness and felicity consist,—not the kind of happiness which is approved and praised by the foolish lovers of this world, but such as the good and faithful of Christ look for, and of which the spiritual and pure in heart, whose conversation is in Heaven, sometimes enjoy a foretaste.

Vain and brief is all human consolation.

Blessed and true is that solace which is felt within from the Truth.

A devout man carries with him everywhere

Jesus, his Comforter, and says to Him, 'Be with me, O Lord Jesus, in every place and at all times.'

'Let this be my consolation, to be quite willing to be without all human relief.'

'And if Thy consolation be wanting, let Thy will and the trial I justly undergo, be for me my highest comfort.'

'For Thou wilt not always be angry, neither shall Thy wrath hang over me for ever.'

CHAPTER XVII.

That all Cares should be cast upon God.

1. MY son, suffer Me to do as I please with you; I know what is best for you.

You think as man, in many things you judge according to human feelings.

O Lord, it is true what Thou sayest. Thou hast greater anxiety for me than all the care I can bestow upon myself.

For he stands very insecurely who does not cast all his care upon Thee.

O Lord, provided only my will may remain right and firm on Thee, do with me whatsoever it shall please Thee.

For whatsoever Thou shalt do with me, it can be nothing but good.

2. If it be Thy will that I should be in darkness, be Thou blessed; and if it be Thy will that I should be in light, be Thou again blessed.

If Thou deign to comfort me, be Thou blessed; and if Thou wilt that I should be in trouble, be Thou ever equally blessed.

My son, this ought to be your state, if you desire to walk with Me.

You ought to be ready to suffer as well as to rejoice.

You ought as willingly to be poor and needy as to be full and rich.

3. O Lord, cheerfully for Thy sake will I suffer whatever you may will to send me.

From Thy hand I am willing to receive indifferently good and evil, sweet and bitter, joy and sorrow, and for all that happens to me to give thanks.

Keep me from all sin, and I shall fear neither death nor hell.

Only cast me not away for ever, nor blot me out of the book of life; and whatever tribulation may come upon me, it shall not hurt me.

CHAPTER XVIII.

That temporal Miseries are to be borne patiently, after the Example of Christ.

1. SON, I came down from Heaven for thy salvation; I took upon Myself thy miseries, not from necessity but drawn by love, that you may learn to be patient and to bear meekly the miseries of this life.

For from the home of My birth, even to My death upon the Cross, I was never free from sorrow.

Of temporal things I endured great want; I frequently heard complaints against Myself; I bore meekly shame and reproach; I received ingratitude in return for benefits; for miracles, blasphemies; for doctrine, reproach.

2. O Lord, since Thou wast patient in Thy life, and in this way especially fulfilled the commandment of Thy Father, it is reasonable that I, a miserable sinner, should bear myself patiently according to Thy will, and as long as Thou willest bear the burden of this corruptible life for my salvation.

For although this present life is felt to be burdensome, yet already by Thy grace it is made very meritorious; and by Thy example and the footsteps of Thy Saints it is rendered more supportable, and more clear to the weak.

It is, too, much more full of consolation than formerly it was in the time of the Old Testament, when the gate of heaven remained closed; and the way itself seemed more obscure, when so few were concerned to seek after the Kingdom of Heaven.

For not even could they, who then were righteous and were to be saved, enter the Heavenly Kingdom before Thy Passion, and the satisfaction of Thy Holy Death.

3. O what thanks am I bound to pay Thee, because Thou hast vouchsafed to shew to me and to all the faithful the right and the good way to Thine eternal Kingdom.

For Thy life is our way, and by holy patience we advance towards Thee, Who art our Crown.

Unless Thou hadst preceded us, and taught us, who would have cared to follow?

Alas, how many would remain far behind, did they not contemplate Thy magnificent example!

Behold, as it is, we are yet lukewarm, though we have before us so many of Thy miracles and sayings.

Where should we be if we had not all this light to aid us in following Thee!

CHAPTER XIX.

On bearing Injuries, and of the proof of a truly patient Man.

1. WHAT is it you say, My son? cease to complain as you consider My Passion and the sufferings of My Saints.

You have "not yet resisted unto blood."

Your sufferings are little in comparison with the sufferings of those who bore so much, who were so strongly tempted, were so grievously afflicted, so variously tried and exercised.

You ought, then, to recall to mind the heavier trials of others, that you may bear more lightly your own little troubles.

And if they do not seem very small to you, take care that it be not your impatience which magnifies them.

Whether, however, they are small or great, try to bear all with patience.

2. The better you dispose yourself for suffering, the more wisely you act, and the richer will be your reward.

You will bear it more easily, if you have diligently trained yourself in mind and habit for that purpose.

Do not say, 'I cannot bear to suffer such treatment from such a man, nor ought I to endure such things as these, for he has done me a grievous wrong, and reproaches me with things I never thought of; but at the hands of some one else I would bear it willingly, and as much as I should think I ought to bear.'

Such a thought is foolish, and does not take into account the nature of patience nor by whom it is to be crowned; but weighs rather the persons, and the injuries which are done.

3. He is not truly patient, who is not willing to suffer except what seems right to himself, and from the person whom he selects.

But the truly patient man does not consider by whom he is tried, whether by a superior, equal, or inferior; whether by a good and holy man, or by one who is perverse and unworthy; but indifferently from all creatures, every affliction which happens to him, however great or frequent it may be, he thankfully receives it from the hand of God, and regards it as a great gain; because nothing before God, however small it may be, which is suffered for God's sake, can pass away without its reward.

4. Be therefore ready for battle, if you wish to win the victory.

Without a conflict you cannot obtain the crown of patience.

But if you desire to be crowned, strive manfully, bear patiently.

Without toil you cannot arrive at rest, nor without a battle can you attain to victory.

5. Make that possible to me, O Lord, by grace, which appears impossible to me by nature.

Thou knowest how little I am able to bear, and how soon I am cast down, when a slight trouble arises.

Let every discipline of tribulation be accepted by me in the spirit of love, for Thy Name's sake; for to suffer pain or trouble for Thee is very beneficial for my soul.

CHAPTER XX.

Of the acknowledgment of our own Infirmity; and of the Miseries of this Life.

1. I WILL confess against myself my unrighteousness; I will confess to Thee my weakness, O Lord.

It is often a small matter which casts me down and saddens me.

I propose to myself to act bravely, but when a small temptation comes, I am at once in great perplexity.

Sometimes it is a very trifling thing which gives rise to a great temptation.

Whilst I think myself fairly safe, before I am

aware of it, I find myself sometimes almost overcome by a slight breath of wind.

2. Behold, therefore, O Lord, my low estate, and my feebleness, which is on all sides known unto Thee.

Have mercy upon me, and draw me out of the mire, that I may not stick fast in it, and may not remain cast down for ever.

It is this which frequently throws me back, and confounds me in Thy presence, that I am so liable to fall, and so weak in resisting my passions.

And if I do not altogether consent, yet their assaults are still troublesome and grievous unto me; and it is very wearisome to live thus daily in conflict.

From this my weakness is made known to me, because hateful imaginations always rush into my mind much more easily than they depart from it.

3. O most mighty God of Israel, zealous Lover of faithful souls! O that Thou wouldest look upon the labour and sorrow of Thy servant, and aid him in all things which he may be called to undertake.

Strengthen me with power from on high, lest the old man, the miserable flesh, not as yet made subject to the spirit, gain dominion over the spirit; against which result I must contend, as long as I breathe in this most miserable life.

Alas, what a life is this, in which are never wanting tribulation and misery; where all things are full of snares and enemies!

For when one trouble or temptation ceases, another takes its place; and when it does not cease, many others unexpectedly supervene.

4. And how is it life is loved when it has so many embitterments, and is subject to so many calamities and miseries?

How indeed can it be called life, when it brings forth so many deaths and so many plagues?

And yet it is loved, and many seek in it all their delight.

The world is often reproached for being deceptive and vain, yet it is not easily forsaken, because the lusts of the flesh bear rule.

But some things induce us to love the world, others to despise it.

The lust of the flesh, the lust of the eyes, and the pride of life draw us to love the world; but the punishments and miseries, which justly follow the gratification of these lusts, excite a hatred of the world and a loathing of it.

But, alas, a depraved taste for pleasure overcomes the mind which is given up to the world, so that it is reckoned a pleasure to be "under the nettles," because the sweetness of God, and the inward delight which accompanies virtue, have been neither felt nor enjoyed.

But those who thoroughly despise the world, and study to live to God in holy discipline, are not ignorant of the Divine sweetness which has been promised to all who truly renounce the world; and they see how grievously the world errs, and how in various ways it is deceived.

CHAPTER XXI.

That we must find our Rest in God, above all good things and gifts.

1. ABOVE all and in all do thou, my soul, rest in the Lord always, for He Himself is the eternal Rest of His Saints.

Grant me, O most sweet and loving Jesus, to rest in Thee above every creature, above all health and beauty, above all glory and honour, above all power and dignity, above all knowledge and shrewdness, above all riches and arts, above all joy and exultation, above all fame and praise, above all sweetness and consolation, above all hope and promise, above all desert and desire, above all gifts and presents which Thou art able to bestow or infuse, above all joy and gladness which the mind is capable of receiving and feeling; finally, above Angels and Archangels, and above all the host of Heaven, above all things visible and invisible, and above all that Thou art not, O my God.

2. Because Thou, O my God, art supremely good above all; Thou only art most High; Thou only art most powerful; Thou only art most rich and self-sufficient; Thou only art most sweet and full of consolation; Thou only art most lovely and most loving; Thou only art most noble and glorious above all things, in Whom all good things are, were, and ever shall be, in perfection.

And, therefore, whatever Thou givest me is small and insufficient, unless Thou givest me Thyself; and what Thou revealest or promisest concerning Thyself does not satisfy, whilst Thou Thyself art neither seen nor fully possessed.

For indeed my heart cannot truly rest, nor be entirely contented, unless it finds its rest in Thee, and mounts above all gifts and above all creatures.

3. O my dearest Spouse, Jesus Christ, O most pure Lover, Ruler of all creation, who will give me wings of true liberty, so that I may fly to Thee and rest in Thee?

O when shall it be granted me ever to wait on Thee alone, and to taste Thy sweetness, O Lord my God?

When shall I fully gain the spirit of recollection, so that on account of Thy love I shall not think of myself, but of Thee alone, to such a degree as to be above all feeling, and in a manner beyond all ordinary experience?

But now I frequently groan, and bear with sorrow my misery.

Because many evils occur in this vale of misery, which often disturb me, sadden and overcloud me; often hinder and distract, allure and entangle me; so that I have no free access to Thee, and cannot enjoy Thy sweet embraces, which are ever within the reach of the blessed spirits.

Let my longings, and my manifold desolations on the earth, move Thee.

4. O Jesus, the Brightness of Eternal Glory, Solace of my soul in its pilgrimage, I raise my mouth to Thee without utterance, and my silence addresses Thee.

How long will my Lord delay His coming?

May He come to me, His poor servant, and make me glad; let Him stretch out His hand and rescue me, miserable as I am, from all my anguish.

Come, O come, for no day or hour can have any peace without Thy Presence, for Thou art my Joy, and without Thee my table is empty.

I am wretched, and like a prisoner who is bound hand and foot, until Thou by the light of Thy Presence dost refresh me, and dost give me freedom, and look with favour upon me.

5. Let others seek what they like instead of Thee, but I for my part delight in nothing but in Thee, my God, my Hope, my Everlasting Salvation.

I will not be silent, nor cease to pray, until Thy grace return to me, and Thou speak inwardly to me.

6. "Behold, here I am; lo, I come to thee, because thou hast called Me. Thy tears, and the desire of thy soul, thy humiliation and thy contrition of heart, have inclined Me and brought Me to thee."

7. And I said, 'Lord, I have called upon Thee, and have desired to enjoy Thee, and am ready to despise all things for Thy sake.

For Thou first didst stir me up to seek Thee; be Thou therefore Blessed, O Lord, Who, according to the multitude of Thy mercies, hast dealt thus graciously with Thy servant.'

What else has Thy servant, O Lord, to say before Thee, unless it be to humble himself deeply in Thy sight, and be ever mindful of his personal sins, his weakness and depravity.

For there is none like unto Thee amongst all the wonders of heaven and earth.

Thy works are very good, O Lord; Thy judgments are true, and Thy Providence governs the universe.

Praise therefore and glory be to Thee, O Wisdom of the Father; let my mouth, my soul, and all created things together, praise and bless Thee.

CHAPTER XXII.

Of the Remembrance of the many Benefits of God.

1. OPEN, O Lord, my heart to Thy law, and teach me to walk in Thy commandments.

Grant me to know Thy will, and to call to mind, with much reverence and careful consideration, Thy benefits, one by one as well as altogether, in order that I may be able to give thanks for them.

But I know and confess, that for the least of them I am unable to pay Thee an adequate tribute of thanksgiving.

I am less than any of the blessings which Thou dost pour upon me; and when I consider Thy generosity, my spirit faints at the thought of its greatness.

2. All that we have in soul and body, whatever we possess, outwardly and inwardly, naturally and supernaturally, are Thy benefits,

and proclaim Thee to be beneficent, kind, and good, from Whom we have received all good things.

And if one has more, another less, yet all is from Thee, and without Thee the least thing cannot be held.

He who has received the greater blessings cannot boast of his own merit, nor be extolled above others, nor deride another who is less favoured; because it is the man who ascribes less to himself, and in his gratitude is more humble and fervent, who is really the greater and the better.

And he who counts himself viler than all men, and judges himself to be more unworthy than others, is the one who is most fit to receive greater blessings.

3. But he who has received fewer gifts ought not to be out of heart, nor to bear it in an indignant spirit, nor to envy him who is richer; but rather to wait on Thee, and highly extol Thy goodness, for that Thou bestowest Thy gifts so abundantly, so freely, so willingly, without respect of persons.

All things come from Thee, and on that account Thou art to be praised for all.

Thou knowest what is expedient for each one to receive; and why one should have more and another less, it is not for us to judge, but for

Thee, by Whom are determined the deserts of each.

4. Wherefore, O Lord God, I even regard it a great blessing, not to possess many gifts which outwardly and according to men seem worthy of praise and renown; so that a person at the thought of his poverty and vileness not only should not be heavy, sad, or dejected, but on the contrary should feel comfort and great delight.

For Thou, O God, hast chosen the poor and the humble, and those who are despised by the world, to be Thy familiar friends and attendants.

Thy Apostles are witnesses, whom Thou hast made princes over all the earth.

For their conversation in the world was without reproach, so humble and simple were they, and without any malice and guile, that they even rejoiced to suffer shame for Thy Name, and what the world flies from they embraced with great affection.

5. Nothing, therefore, ought to gladden one who loves Thee and recognises Thy benefits, so much as the fulfilment of Thy will in him, and the good pleasure of Thy eternal appointment, with which he should be so contented and comforted, that he would as readily be the least, as another would wish to be the greatest;

he would, too, be as peaceable and happy in the last place as in the first; as willing to be despised and of no account, having neither name nor fame, as to be honoured before others and greater than others in the world.

For Thy will and the love of Thy honour would be his highest consideration, and would bring him more comfort and gratification than all the benefits he has ever, or will ever receive.

CHAPTER XXIII.

Of Four Things which bring Great Peace.

1. MY son, I will now teach you the way of peace and of true liberty.

2. Do, Lord, what Thou sayest, for I shall be glad to hear it.

3. Study, My son, to do the will of another in preference to doing your own will.

Choose always to have less rather than more.

Seek always the lower place, and to be under all.

Always desire and pray that the Will of God may be wholly accomplished in you.

Behold, the man who follows these maxims enters within the borders of peace and rest.

4. O Lord, this short discourse of Thine contains much perfection.

It is short in words, but full of meaning, and rich in fruit.

For if I could faithfully observe it, I should not so easily be disturbed.

For whenever I find myself troubled and burdened, I discover that I have departed from this instruction.

But Thou Who canst do all things, and always lovest that my soul should progress, increase in me Thy grace, that I may be able to carry out what Thou teachest, and to work out my salvation.

Prayer

Against evil Thoughts.

5. O Lord, my God, be not Thou far from me; my God, look upon me and help me, for in me various thoughts have arisen, and great fears afflict my soul.

How shall I pass through this unhurt? how shall I break them away?

6. 'I,' saith He, 'will go before thee, and will humble the great ones of the earth.

I will open the gates of the prison, and will reveal to thee hidden secrets.'

7. Do, O Lord, what Thou sayest, and cause all evil thoughts to fly before Thy face.

This is my hope and my only consolation, to

fly to Thee in every trouble, to trust in Thee, to call upon Thee from my inmost heart, and patiently to wait for Thy consolation.

Prayer

For Illumination of Mind.

8. Enlighten me, O good Jesus, with the brightness of Thy eternal light, and scatter all darkness from the recesses of my heart.

Restrain my many wandering thoughts, and dash away those temptations which come violently against me.

Fight for me strongly, and drive away the evil beasts—for I give the alluring lusts of the flesh that name; that peace may be brought about by Thy power, and that abundance of praise may resound to Thee in Thy holy court, that is, in a pure conscience.

Command the winds and the storms; say to the sea, be still; say to the north wind, blow not; and there shall be a great calm.

9. Send out Thy light, and Thy truth, that they may shine upon the earth, for earth am I without form and void, until Thou enlightenest me.

Pour forth Thy grace from above, fill my heart with heavenly dew, supply rivers of devotion to water the face of the earth, that it may bring forth good fruit and the best.

Lift up my mind, which is weighed down by the burden of my sins, and draw up my whole desire to heavenly things; so that having tasted the sweetness of the happiness which is from above, I may find the contemplation of earthly things to be a weariness.

10. Snatch me and rescue me from all the fleeting consolations of the creature, for no created thing is able fully to quiet and console my longings.

Unite me to Thyself with an inseparable bond of love; since Thou Alone dost satisfy Thy loving one, and apart from Thee all things are empty.

CHAPTER XXIV.

Of avoiding Curiosity and Inquisitiveness respecting the Lives of others.

1. MY son, be not curious, nor concern yourself with useless anxieties.

What is this or that to thee? 'Follow thou Me.'

For what is it to you, whether that man be such or such, or whether this man do or speak this or that?

You are not required to answer for others,

but to give an account of your own self. Why then do you involve yourself with others?

Behold, I know all men, and I see all things which are done under the sun, and I know how it fares with each one, what he thinks, what he wills, and what is the drift of his intention.

To Me therefore all things are to be committed; but do you preserve for yourself the blessing of peace, and leave the disturber to disturb as he will.

It shall come upon him, whatever he has done or said, for he cannot deceive Me.

2. Be not careful for the mere shadow of a great name, nor for the intimacy of many persons, nor for the private affection of men; for these things produce distractions and great darkness in the heart.

I would gladly declare My word to you, and reveal to you hidden things, if you would diligently observe My coming, and open for Me the door of your heart.

Be 'sober, and watch unto prayer,' and be humble at all times.

CHAPTER XXV.

In what firm Peace of Heart and true Progress do consist.

1. MY son, I have said, 'Peace I leave with you, My peace I give unto you: not as the world giveth, give I unto you.'

Every one desires peace, but every one does not consider what brings true peace.

My peace is with the lowly and meek in heart; thy peace shall be in much patience.

If thou wilt hear Me and follow My voice, thou shalt be able to enjoy much peace.

What shall I do, Lord?

In every thing look to yourself, both in what you do, and in what you say, and always make it your aim to please Me only, and neither to desire nor to seek any thing out of Me.

But concerning the sayings and doings of others judge nothing rashly, neither meddle with things which are not entrusted to you; then it will be possible that you may be seldom or little disturbed.

2. But never to feel any disturbance, nor to suffer any trouble of mind or body, is not to be looked for in our present condition, but in the unbroken rest of eternity.

Therefore do not think that you have already

found the true peace, because at present you feel no heaviness; neither imagine that at present all is well, if you are not vexed by any enemy; nor that perfection is attained, if all things take place according to your inclination.

Neither think much of yourself, nor consider yourself especially beloved, if you have a feeling of great devotion and sweetness; for these things are not the distinguishing mark of a true lover of virtue, neither does the progress or perfection of a man consist in such things.

3. In what, then, does it consist, O Lord?

In giving up yourself with all your heart to the Divine Will, not seeking the things which are your own, either in little or great, either in time or in eternity; so that, weighing all things with an equal balance, you may, without changing the expression of your face, always give thanks both in prosperity and adversity.

If you were so courageous and patient in hope, that when inward consolation is withdrawn, you could prepare your heart for greater suffering still; and if, instead of justifying yourself as not deserving to be so afflicted, you rather acknowledged the justice of all My appointments for you, and praised My Holy Name, then would you walk in the true and right path of peace, and your hope would remain unshaken that you should soon again see My Face with joy.

But if you attain to a complete contempt of yourself, know that then you shall enjoy abundance of peace, as much as is possible in your earthly pilgrimage.

CHAPTER XXVI.

Of the Excellence of a Free Mind, which is gained more by humble Prayer than by Study.

1. O LORD, this is the work of a perfect man, never to relax his mind from the contemplation of heavenly objects, and to pass amidst many cares as though he had no cares, not in a stolid manner, but with that special prerogative of a free mind—detachment from all inordinate affection to created things.

2. I beseech Thee, my most gracious God, preserve me from the cares of this life, lest I should be too much taken up with them; from the many necessities of the body, lest I should be ensnared by pleasure; and from all the hindrances to my soul, lest, broken by troubles, I should be cast down.

I do not speak of those things which worldly vanity so eagerly seeks, but of those miseries and penalties which weigh down and retard the soul of Thy servant through the common curse of mortality, so that it is unable to obtain liberty of spirit as often as it would.

3. O my God, Thou Sweetness Unspeakable, turn for me into bitterness all carnal delight which draws me away from the love of eternal things, and attracts me to itself on account of its offer of present enjoyment; let it not conquer me, O Lord; let not flesh and blood conquer me; let not the world deceive me, and its fleeting glory; let not the Devil by his subtlety cast me down.

Give me strength to resist, patience to endure, constancy to persevere.

Grant me instead of all the joys of this world the sweetest unction of Thy Spirit; and instead of carnal love infuse into me the love of Thy Name.

4. Behold! food, drink, clothes, and all else that pertains to the support of the body, are burdensome to the fervent spirit.

Grant that I may use such supports with moderation, and not care too much about them.

To do without anything cannot be, for nature must be sustained; but the holy law forbids us to seek superfluities, and luxuries; for did we do so, the flesh would rebel against the spirit.

In these things let Thy Hand, O Lord, guide and teach me, that I may not at all run into excess.

CHAPTER XXVII.

That it is Self-Love which chiefly hinders us from obtaining the Supreme Good.

1. MY son, you must give all for all, and be in nothing your own.

Know that the love of yourself is more hurtful to you than anything else in the world.

According to your love and affection for any thing so will be your difficulty, more or less, in setting yourself free from it.

If your love were pure, simple, and well-ordered, you would not be in captivity to any thing.

Do not desire what you may not have; do not seek to have what may be a hindrance to you, and may deprive you of inward liberty.

Marvellous is it, that you do not from the very bottom of your heart commit yourself to Me, with all things that you can wish for or have.

2. Why do you pine away with vain grief? why do you weary yourself with needless cares?

Rest in My good will, and you shall suffer no harm.

If you seek this or that, and wish to be here or there for your own convenience, or for the sake of having your own way, you will never be at rest, nor free from anxiety; because in every thing there will be some drawback, and in every place there will be some one to oppose you.

3. Your welfare, therefore, does not lie in your gains or in the increase of external things, but rather in despising them, and in eradicating the desire of them out of your heart.

And this holds good not only of revenues and of riches, but also of the thirst for honour, and of the desire for vain praise—all which things pass away with the world.

Place is but a slight protection, if fervour of spirit is wanting; neither shall that peace stand long which is sought from without, if this condition of heart lack a true foundation, that is, if you do not stand firmly in Me;—you may change, but not for the better.

For when temptation presents itself, and is accepted, you will find what you have fled from, and more too.

A Prayer

For the Cleansing of the Heart and for Heavenly Wisdom.

4. Strengthen me, O God, by the grace of Thy Holy Spirit; grant me to be strengthened with might in the inner man, and to put away from my heart all useless anxiety and distress, and let

me never be drawn aside by various longings after any thing whatever, whether it be worthless or precious; but may I regard all things as passing away, and myself as passing away with them.

For nothing is lasting under the sun, for all things are vanity and vexation of spirit. O, how wise is he who thus regards them!

Grant me, O Lord, heavenly wisdom, that I may learn to seek Thee above all things, and to find Thee, to enjoy and to love Thee above all things, and to understand all other things as they are, according to the order of Thy wisdom.

Grant me prudently to avoid the one who flatters me, and patiently to bear with the one who contradicts me; for it is a mark of great wisdom not to be moved by every wind of words, nor to give ear to the wicked flattery of the siren; for thus we shall go on securely in the course we have begun.

CHAPTER XXVIII.

Against the Tongues of Slanderers.

1. MY son, do not take it amiss if some think badly of you, and say about you what you do not like to hear.

You ought to think worse of yourself, and to believe that no one is weaker than yourself.

If you live an inward life, you will pay but little account to the passing words which are from without.

It is no small wisdom to be silent in the evil time, and to turn inwardly to Me, and not to be troubled by man's judgment.

2. Let not your peace rest in the utterances of men, for whether they put a good or bad construction on your conduct does not make you other than you are.

Where is your true peace and true glory to be found? Is it not in Me?

And he who neither seeks to please men, nor fears to displease them, shall enjoy much peace.

From inordinate affection and vain fear arise all disquietude of heart and distraction of the senses.

CHAPTER XXIX.

How we ought to call upon God, and bless Him when we are in Trouble.

1. BLESSED be Thy name, O Lord, for ever, Who hast been pleased to visit me with this trial and tribulation.

I cannot escape it, but must of necessity turn to Thee as my refuge, that Thou mayest help me and make it profitable to me.

O Lord, I am now in trouble, and my heart is

ill at ease, for I am much tried by the present suffering.

And now, O Beloved Father, what shall I say? I am in a great strait; save me from this hour.

But on this account came I to this hour, that Thou mightest be glorified, when I shall have been greatly humbled, and by Thee delivered.

May it please Thee, O Lord, to deliver me; for, poor as I am, what can I do for myself? and whither shall I go without Thee?

Give me patience, O Lord, even at this crisis.

Help me, O my God, and I will not fear however much I may have to bear.

2.* And now, in the midst of this, what shall I say?

O Lord, let Thy Will be done; I have rightly deserved to be thus troubled and afflicted.

Therefore I ought to bear it, and O that I may be patient until the storm pass away and leave a deeper calm behind it.

But Thine Almighty Hand is able even to take away this temptation from me, and to lessen its violence, so that I may not be thoroughly prostrated by it; as Thou hast often done with me before, O my God! my Mercy!

And the more difficult it is to me, the more easy to Thee, is this change of the right hand of the Most High.

CHAPTER XXX.

Of seeking Divine Assistance, and of Confidence in recovering Grace.

1. MY son, I am the Lord Who gives thee strength in the day of trouble. Come to Me when it is not well with thee.

This is what most of all hinders heavenly consolation, that you are too slow in turning to prayer.

For before you earnestly seek Me, you seek oftentimes many other sources of consolation, and refresh yourself with external things.

And therefore it comes to pass that you get little assistance, until you realize that I am He Who delivers those who trust in Me; and that without Me there is no real help, no profitable counsel, no lasting remedy.

But now, having recovered yourself after the storm, grow strong again in the light of My mercies; for I am near (saith the Lord) to restore all things, not only entirely, but also abundantly, and to add to them.

2. Is there anything hard for Me? or shall I be like one who says but does not do?

Where is your faith? Stand firmly and perseveringly, be patient and brave; comfort shall come to you in due season.

Wait for me, wait; I will come and heal you.

It is a temptation which vexes you, and a vain fear which terrifies you.

What does your anxiety about future events—events which may never happen—bring you but sorrow upon sorrow?

'Sufficient unto the day is the evil thereof.'

It is vain and profitless to entertain either joy or sorrow concerning future things, which perhaps may never come to pass.

3. But man is liable to be deluded with imaginations of this kind; and it is the sign of a mind yet weak, to be so easily drawn aside by the suggestion of the Enemy.

For he does not care whether it is concerning truth or falsehood, that he deceives and mocks you; whether it is by love of the present or by fear of the future, that he overthrows you.

Let not, then, your heart be troubled, neither let it be afraid; trust in Me, and confide in My mercy.

When you think yourself far off from Me, I am often nearest to you.

When you think that almost all is lost, then often the opportunity for much gain is at hand.

All is not lost, when any thing goes contrary to you.

You must not judge according to your present feelings, nor stick fast in any trouble, from whatever quarter it may come; nor receive it, as if all hope of getting over it were taken away.

4. Do not think that you are entirely forsaken, although for a time I may have sent some trouble upon you, or may have withdrawn some consolation, for so it happens to those who are travelling towards the Kingdom of Heaven.

And without doubt it is more expedient for you and the rest of My servants, to be tried in various ways, than to have every thing your own way.

I know your secret thoughts, and that it is very conducive to your salvation, that you should sometimes suffer dryness of spirit, lest perhaps you should be puffed up by prosperity, and flatter yourself that you are what you are not.

What I have given, I can take away; and can restore again, as it pleases Me.

5. When I have given it, it is still Mine; when I have taken it away, I do not take any thing that belongs to you, for "every good gift and every perfect gift" is Mine.

If I send you affliction or any cross whatever, do not assume an injured tone, nor lose heart; because I am able quickly to raise you up again, and to turn all your heaviness into joy.

But I am Just, and greatly to be praised, when I so deal with you.

6. If you are really wise, and if you take a true

view of things, you ought never to give yourself up to despondency because of affliction, but rather to rejoice and give thanks.

Yes, account it a special reason for rejoicing that I afflict you with sorrows, and do not spare you.

'As the Father hath loved Me, I also love you,' I said to My beloved disciples, whom indeed I have not sent forth to temporal joys but to great conflicts; not to honours, but to contempt; not to ease, but to toil; not to rest, but to bring forth much fruit with patience.

My son, remember these words.

CHAPTER XXXI.

Of Setting aside every Created Thing that the Creator may be found.

1. MY Lord, I yet stand in need of greater grace, if I must advance to such a height, as to feel that no created thing has any longer power to hinder me.

For as long as anything holds me back, I cannot freely fly to Thee.

He longed to fly freely to Thee, who said,— 'O, that I had wings like a dove, for then would I flee away and be at rest.'

Who is more at rest than he who has a single

eye to the glory of God? and who is more free than he who desires nothing upon earth?

A man ought, therefore, to pass beyond all created things, and entirely to forsake himself, and with rapt mind to stand and see that the Creator of all things has no creature who is to be compared to Himself.

And unless any one is detached in heart from all created things, he cannot with freedom give himself to Divine things.

For on this account but few are contemplative, because few know how to separate themselves completely from transitory and created objects.

2. To obtain this, great grace is required, that it may elevate the soul and raise it above itself.

And if a man is not lifted up above himself in spirit, and freed from all creatures, and wholly united to God, it does not matter much what he knows or what he has.

Long will he be small, and will grovel in the dust, who reckons anything great but the One, Infinite, Eternal Good.

And whatever is not God is nothing, and ought to be regarded as nothing.

There is a great difference, indeed, between the wisdom of an illuminated and devout man, and the knowledge of a literary man or studious divine.

Much more noble is the wisdom which is from above and from the Divine influence, than that which is laboriously acquired by the human intellect.

3. Many are found who desire contemplation, but they will not strive to practise those things which are necessary for the attainment of it.

The great impediment is, that men rest in signs and things of sense, and neglect the entire mortification of themselves.

I know not how it is, nor what induces us, nor what we pretend to, that we who have the name of spiritual persons bestow all our labour, and very much of our care, on things which are transitory and worthless, and scarcely ever gather ourselves up to think about our own inward life.

4. Alas, after recalling ourselves for a moment, we rush off to outward things again, and do not subject our works to a diligent examination.

We do not consider where we are setting our affections, neither do we deplore the lack of purity in all our actions.

Because 'all flesh had corrupted his way upon the earth,' therefore came the great flood.

Since, therefore, our inward affection is corrupt, it necessarily follows that the action should —as the index of the lack of inward moral vigour —be corrupt also.

Out of a pure heart proceeds the fruit of a good life.

5. We inquire how much a man has done, but with what dispositions the work is done is not so carefully considered.

We ask whether a man is brave, rich, handsome, clever, a good writer, a good singer, or a good workman; but how poor he is in spirit, how patient and meek, how devout and spiritual, is what few speak of.

Nature respects the outer man: grace turns itself to the inner man. The former is often in error, the latter trusts in God, so that there may be no mistake.

CHAPTER XXXII.

Of Self Denial and the Renunciation of every Corrupt Desire.

1. MY son, you cannot have perfect liberty, unless you entirely deny yourself.

All self-seekers, and lovers of self; all covetous, anxious persons; and all those who wander about and are ever in quest of ease and comfort, and not of the things of Jesus Christ, are in bondage.

These often plan and devise things which will not stand, for every thing that is not of God shall perish.

Hold fast this short and summary saying—"Forsake all, and you shall find all; leave your desires, and you shall find rest."

Give your mind to this, and when you have put it into practice, you shall understand all things.

2. O Lord, this is not the work of a day nor child's play; indeed, in this short sentence all Religious perfection is summed up.

3. My son, you ought not to be turned aside, nor at once cast down, when you hear what is the way of the perfect; but rather be stirred up to higher things, or at least to pant with desire for them.

Would that it were so with you, and that you had reached such a point as to be no longer a lover of self, but that you were willing simply to obey My bidding and that of your appointed spiritual father; then you would indeed please Me, and you would pass all your life in joy and peace.

You have yet many things to forsake, and unless they are entirely given up to Me, you will not obtain what you seek.

I counsel thee to buy of Me gold tried in the fire, that thou mayest become rich, that is, heavenly wisdom, which treads under foot all that is base.

Disregard all earthly wisdom, and all concern to please men and yourself.

4. I have said, that you must buy for yourself things low and contemptible in human estimation, instead of those which are accounted precious and high.

For heavenly wisdom is indeed in the eyes of men worthless, of little account, and almost ignored, in that it exalts not self, nor seeks to be magnified on the earth.

Many indeed proclaim it with their mouth, but are far from it in their life, yet it is the pearl of great price which but few find.

CHAPTER XXXIII.

On the Changeableness of the Heart, and on Directing our Final Intention towards God.

1. MY son, do not trust to your feelings, for whatever they may be at present they are liable soon to become different.

As long as you live you will be subject to change, even against your will; so that you will be found at one time merry, at another sad; at one time peaceful, at another disturbed; at one time devotional, at another with distaste for devotion; at one time diligent, at another sluggish; at one time grave, at another light.

But he who is wise and well-instructed in spirit stands above these fluctuations, not minding what he feels in himself, nor which way the wind of natural instability blows; but only that the whole bent of his soul might be set towards the right and the best end.

For thus he will be able to remain one and the same and unshaken, if he keeps, through so many changing events, the eye of his intention simply and constantly directed towards Me.

2. But the greater the purity of the intention is, the greater will be the constancy with which you will pass through the various storms.

In many, however, the eye of pure intention is weak, for it quickly looks at some pleasure which meets it; and seldom is any one found who is entirely free from the stain of some self-seeking.

Thus of old the Jews came to Bethany to Martha and Mary, not for Jesus' sake only, but that they might see Lazarus also.

Therefore the eye of the intention must be cleansed, that it may become simple and right, and may be, through all the various intervening objects, directed to Me.

CHAPTER XXXIV.

That God is Sweet above All and in All Things to him who loves Him

1. BEHOLD my God, and my all! What can I wish more? and what greater happiness can I desire?

O word of sweet savour and delightful! but only to him who loves the Word, not the world, nor the things that are in the world.

'My God and my all!' To him who understands, this saying is enough; and to say it over and over again, is delightful to him who loves.

If Thou art present all things are delightful, but if Thou art absent all things are wearisome.

Thou makest the heart to be tranquil, and givest great peace and festive joy.

Thou makest us to think well of all, and to praise Thee in all circumstances; and nothing without Thee can afford any lasting pleasure; but if any thing is to be pleasant and delightful, Thy grace must accompany it, and Thy wisdom must impart a relish to it.

2. He who has a relish for Thee, will he not find sweetness in everything? and he who has no relish for Thee, what can be sweet to him?

But the wise of this world, and those who mind the things of the flesh, are wanting in Thy wisdom; for in the former there is nothing but vanity, and in the latter death.

But those who despise the world and mortify the flesh are found to be indeed wise, because they leave vanity for truth, the flesh for the spirit.

These delight in God; and whatever good is found in the creatures, they wholly refer to the praise of their Maker.

But great, ah, very great, is the difference between the sweetness of the Creator and of the creature, of eternity and of time, of the Light Uncreated and the light imparted.

3. O Light Eternal, transcending all created lights, dart Thy bright beams from above, and penetrate the inmost recesses of my heart.

Cleanse, gladden, brighten, and enliven my spirit with all its powers, that I may cleave to Thee with ecstasies of joy.

O, when shall that blessed and longed-for hour arrive, when Thou wilt satisfy me with Thy Presence, and be to me All in all!

Until this is granted to me, my joy will not be full.

Alas! the old man still lives in me—is not yet entirely crucified, is not yet completely dead; he still lusts strongly against the spirit. The inner war goes on, and the kingdom of my soul is not suffered to be at rest.

4. But Thou Who stillest the raging of the sea, and subduest the violence of the waves, arise and help me.

Scatter the nations that delight in war; crush them in Thy might.

Shew forth, I beseech Thee, Thy wonderful works, and let Thy right hand be glorified, for I have no other hope or refuge but in Thee, O Lord my God.

CHAPTER XXXV.

That there is no Security from Temptation in this Life.

1. MY son, you are never secure in this life, but as long as you live you will always be in need of spiritual armour.

You are in the midst of enemies, and they will attack you on the right hand and on the left.

If therefore you do not employ on all sides the shield of patience, you will soon be wounded.

Moreover, if you do not fix your heart on Me with the sincere desire of suffering all things for My sake, you will never be able to sustain the heat of the conflict, nor to attain to the palm of the Blessed.

Therefore you ought manfully to struggle

through all, and with a firm hand to deal with the obstacles which are in your path. .

For to him that overcometh is the manna given, and to him that ceases to struggle is reserved much misery.

2. If you seek rest in this life, how then will you come to the eternal Rest?

You must now seek not much rest, but great patience.

Seek true peace, not on earth, but in Heaven; not in men, nor in any other creature, but in God alone.

For the love of God you ought to be ready to undergo all things, that is to say, all labours, sorrows, trials, vexations, distresses, necessities, infirmities, injuries, reproaches, reproofs, humiliations, shame, corrections and contempt.

These are the things which aid us in forming virtues; these things are the tests of the young disciple of Christ; these things weave the heavenly crown.

I will reward you eternally for your short labour, and with infinite glory for transient shame.

3. Do you think that you will always have spiritual consolations whenever you please?

My Saints did not always have them, but had many afflictions, and different kinds of temptation, and great spiritual desolation.

But they bore all patiently, and trusted rather in God than in themselves; knowing that the sufferings of this time are not worthy to be compared to the reward of future glory.

Do you wish to have at once that, which others after many tears and great labours have with difficulty won?

Wait for the Lord, act manfully and be of good courage; be not distrustful, and do not give way, but lay out body and soul continually for the glory of God.

I will reward you most abundantly, and be with you in every trial.

CHAPTER XXXVI.

Against the vain Judgments of Men.

1. MY son, rest your heart firmly on the Lord, and do not fear the judgment which man may pass on you, when your conscience declares you to be dutiful and innocent.

It is good and blessed to suffer in this way, nor will it be oppressive to the heart which is humble, and which trusts rather in God than in itself.

Many talk much, and therefore little trust is to be put in what they say.

Besides, it is not possible to satisfy all.

And if Paul did try to please all in the Lord, and to make himself all things to all men, yet he also counted it a very small thing that he should be judged of man's judgment.

2. He laboured for the edification and salvation of others to the utmost of his power, yet he could not avoid being sometimes judged or despised by others.

Therefore he committed all to God, to Whom all things are manifest, and by patience and humility defended himself against the tongues of those who spoke unjustly, and of those who devised vain and false charges, and of those who threw out accusations of whatever kind they wished.

Sometimes, however, he rebutted the charge, lest on account of his silence there should arise an occasion of scandal to the weak.

3. Who art thou, that thou shouldest be afraid of a mortal man? To-day he is, and to-morrow he is gone.

Fear God, and you will have no occasion to fear man.

What harm can any man do you either by his words or offensive actions? He will do more harm to himself than to you, and will not himself be able, whoever he may be, to escape the judgment of God.

Keep God before your eyes, and do not contend in a quarrellous manner.

But if for once you seem to be beaten, and to suffer an unmerited exposure to shame, do not become indignant, nor lessen your crown through impatience.

But rather lift up your eyes to Me in Heaven, Who am able to deliver you from all shame and wrong, and to reward every one according to his works.

CHAPTER XXXVII.

Of Pure and Entire Resignation of one's self for the obtaining Freedom of Heart.

1. MY son, forsake yourself, and you shall find Me.

Have no choice, and regard nothing as your own, and you shall always gain.

For a greater measure of grace is granted to you, the moment you have given yourself up, and not returned to self again.

2. O Lord, how often shall I resign myself, and in what shall I resign myself?

3. Always and on all occasions; as in little so also in much. I allow no reserves, but in all things I will that you should be divested of self-seeking.

How otherwise can you be Mine, and I thine, unless you have been inwardly and outwardly stripped of all self-will?

The sooner you effect this, the better will it be for you; and the more fully and sincerely it is done, the better you will please Me, and the greater will be your gain.

4. Some resign themselves, but with a certain reserve; for they do not fully trust in God, and therefore are anxious to provide for themselves.

Some there are also who at first offer all, but afterwards through attacks of temptation return to what they had left, and so make no progress in virtue.

These will not arrive at the true liberty of a pure heart, and the grace of a sweet intercourse with Me, unless they first entirely resign themselves and continue to deny themselves daily; without which a blessed union with Me can neither be established, nor be lasting.

5. I have said it often to you, and now say it again,—forsake yourself, resign yourself, and you shall enjoy great inward peace.

Give all for all, ask for nothing, desire no return; abide purely and unhesitatingly in Me, and you shall possess Me.

You shall be free in heart, and darkness shall not cover you.

Aim at this; pray for this; let it be your one

desire, that you may be entirely stripped of all selfish motives, and thus naked may follow Jesus naked—dying to self, and living eternally to Me.

Then shall all vain fancies cease, all risings of evil, and superfluous cares.

Then, too, shall immoderate fear depart, and inordinate love shall die.

CHAPTER XXXVIII.

Of Ruling ourselves well as to the Outer Life, and of recourse to God in Dangers.

1. MY son, you ought to aim diligently at this, that, in every place, action, and outward employment you may be inwardly free and self-controlled; and that all things may be under you, and not you under them.

That you may be lord and master of your own actions, and not a slave or hireling.

But rather be a freed man and a true Hebrew, one of those who are translated into the lot and liberty of the children of God; who rise above the present, and contemplate the eternal; who regard things transitory with the left, but things celestial with the right eye; who are not dragged down by temporal things, but who, by making good use of them, lead them to the end for which they were ordained by God, according to

His plan, Who is the Supreme Artificer, and who leaves nothing without its purpose and place in His creation.

2. But if you in every event do not depend upon the outward appearance, and do not measure with a carnal eye what you see and hear, but at once in every case enter like Moses into the tabernacle to consult the Lord, you shall sometimes hear a Divine response, and shall return instructed about many things, present and future.

For Moses always had recourse to the tabernacle to settle doubts and questions, and fled to the aid of prayer when he wanted strength to meet dangers and to withstand human depravity.

And so you ought to fly for refuge into the secret place of your heart, most fervently imploring Divine help.

For therefore Joshua and the Children of Israel are said to have been deceived by the Gibeonites, because they did not first seek counsel at the mouth of the Lord, but putting too much reliance on fair words, they were deceived by a pretended piety.

CHAPTER XXXIX.

That a Man must not be over Eager about his Affairs.

1. MY son, commit your cause always to Me; I will manage it well at the right time.
Wait for My ordering of it, and you shall thereby find that you make progress.

2. O Lord, I willingly enough commit all things to Thee, for my anxiety is of little avail.
O that I did not cling so much to plans for the future, but yielded myself up unhesitatingly to Thy good pleasure.

3. My son, often a man hotly pursues something which he desires, but when he has gained it, he begins to feel differently; for the affections are not wont to remain long on one object, but rather urge us on from one thing to another.
It is, therefore, of no small importance to forsake self even in the smallest things.

4. A man's real spiritual advancement consists in the denying of himself, and the man who has formed the habit of self-denial is very much at liberty and is secure.
But the old Enemy—adversary of all that is good—does not cease from temptation, and day and night is constructing deep pitfalls, if per-

chance he may be able to precipitate the unwary into the deceitful snare.

'Watch and pray,' saith the Lord, 'that ye enter not into temptation.'

CHAPTER XL.

That a Man has nothing Good of Himself, nor any thing whereof to Glory.

1. 'LORD, what is man, that Thou art mindful of him, or the son of man, that Thou visitest him?'

What has man deserved, that Thou shouldest give him Thy grace?

O Lord, what grounds have I for complaint, if Thou forsake me? or what can I allege, if Thou do not grant my request?

This certainly I may truly think and say, 'O Lord, I am nothing, I can do nothing, I have nothing good of myself, but am deficient in everything, and I ever tend to nothing.'

And unless I am upheld by Thee, and inwardly instructed, I become altogether lukewarm and lax.

2. But Thou, O Lord, art always the same, and endurest for ever; Thou art always Good, Just, and Holy, doing all things well, justly, and holily, and ordering them in wisdom.

But I, who am more prone to fall than to rise, never continue in one state, for I pass through seven different stages of life.

But a change for the better quickly takes place when it is Thy good pleasure, and Thou stretchest forth Thine hand to help; for Thou alone art able to help without human aid, and so to strengthen me that my face shall no more be turned to various objects, but my heart shall be turned to Thee, and find its rest in Thee alone.

3. Wherefore, if I knew well how to cast off all human consolation, either to obtain devotion, or from the necessity whereby I am compelled to seek Thee—all human consolation being insufficient,—then should I have grounds to hope for Thy favour, and to rejoice in Thy gift of new consolation.

4. Thanks be to Thee, from Whom comes every thing that turns out well for me.

But I am vanity, and nothing before Thee—a man changeable and weak.

What is there that I can glory of? or why do I seek for reputation?

Is it not for nothing? yes, it is most empty.

Truly vain-glory is an evil pest, the greatest vanity; because it draws away from true glory, and despoils us of heavenly grace.

For when a man is pleased with himself, he is

displeasing to Thee; whilst he thirsts for human praise, he is depriving himself of real virtues.

5. But true glory and holy rejoicing consist in glorying in Thee, not in himself; in rejoicing in Thy Name, not in his own goodness; and in finding delight in no creature, save for Thy sake.

Let Thy Name be praised, not mine; let Thy work be magnified, not mine; let Thy Name be holy, and let no human praise be turned towards me.

Thou art my glory, Thou art the joy of my heart.

In Thee will I glory and rejoice all the day, but for myself I will not glory at all, unless it be in my infirmities.

6. Let the Jews seek glory one of another, I will seek that which comes from God only.

All human glory indeed, all temporal honour, all worldly elevation, is vanity and folly, when compared to Thy eternal glory.

O my God, my Truth and my Mercy! O Blessed Trinity! To Thee alone be praise, power, honour, and glory throughout infinite ages.

CHAPTER XLI.

Of the Contempt of all Worldly Honour.

1. MY son, do not take it to heart, if you see others honoured and promoted, but yourself despised and humiliated.

Lift up your heart to Me in Heaven, and do not grieve because men despise you on earth.

2. O Lord, we are in darkness, and by vanity are soon misled.

If I rightly saw myself, I could not say that any creature had ever unjustly treated me; and therefore I cannot justly complain before Thee.

But because I have frequently and grievously sinned against Thee, every creature may rightly take arms against me.

To me, therefore, is justly due confusion of face and contempt; but to Thee praise, honour, power and glory.

And unless I am ready and gladly willing to be despised and forsaken by all creatures, and to be regarded as altogether nothing, I cannot be inwardly at peace, nor gain strength and spiritual illumination, nor be fully united to Thee.

CHAPTER XLII.

That our Peace must not depend on Man.

1. MY son, if you rest your peace on any person, because he is after your own heart, or for the pleasure of his companionship, you will be unsettled and anxious.

But if you have recourse to the ever-living and abiding Truth, when a friend goes away or dies you will not be overwhelmed with grief.

In Me the love of your friend ought to stand; and whoever seems good, and very dear to you in this life, ought to be loved for My sake.

Friendship apart from Me is of no value, and cannot last; nor is that union of love genuine and pure which is not knit together by Me.

You ought to be so dead to the deep attachments of chosen friends, that, as far as in you lies, you should long for no human companionship.

The nearer a man draws to God, the further he withdraws himself from all earthly comforts.

So much the higher he will ascend towards God, as he descends the lower into himself, and becomes the viler in his own sight.

2. But he who attributes any thing good to himself, hinders God's grace from coming to

him; because the grace of the Holy Spirit always seeks a humble heart.

If you could be completely emptied of self, and rid of all attachment to the creature, then might My Presence be shed abroad within you with great grace.

When your face is turned to creatures, the Creator's Face is withdrawn from you.

Learn to conquer yourself in all things for the Creator's sake, and then you will gain a true knowledge of Him.

However little it may be, if anything is loved and cared for inordinately, it detains the soul from the Sovereign Good, and injures it.

CHAPTER XLIII.

Against Vain and Worldly Learning.

1. MY son, let not the fair and subtle sayings of men move you, 'for the Kingdom of God is not in word, but in power.'

Attend to My words, which inflame the heart and enlighten the mind; which prick the conscience, and soothe in manifold ways the wounded spirit.

Never study for the purpose of appearing more wise or learned; but strive to mortify your evil passions, which will be a greater benefit to you than the knowledge of many abstruse matters.

2. When you have read and learnt much, you will have ever to revert to the one First Principle.

I am the One Who teaches men knowledge, and I impart to little ones a clearer knowledge than can be taught by man.

He to whom I speak will soon become wise, and wax strong in spirit.

Woe be to them who are curious about the things of this world, and who care little to discover the best way of serving Me.

The time will come when Christ, the Master of masters, the Lord of angels, shall appear to hear the tasks of all, that is to examine the consciences of every one.

And then will He 'search Jerusalem with candles,' and bring to light the hidden things of darkness, and silence the strife of tongues.

3. I in a moment can lift up the humble mind, and make it enter more deeply into the principles of Eternal Truth than if one had studied ten years in the schools.

I teach without the sound of words, without the strife of opinions, without ambition of honour, without the contention of controversy.

I teach man to despise earthly things, to grow

weary of the present, to seek and to taste already the things eternal, to shun honours, to suffer reproaches, to place all hope in Me, to desire nothing out of Me, and above all to love Me with an ardent love.

4. For one, simply by loving Me intensely, learnt Divine mysteries, and gave utterance to them.

He made more progress by forsaking all things, than by studying subtle questions.

But to some I reveal ordinary things, to others I speak more particularly; to some by types and shadows I shew myself sweetly, to others in the full light I reveal mysteries.

The voice which comes from books is one, but the meaning it conveys is not equally comprehended by all, for I am the internal Teacher of Truth, the Searcher of hearts, the Discerner of the thoughts, the Mover of the actions; distributing to every man as I think right.

CHAPTER XLIV.

Of not taking up the Outward Things which come in our Path.

1. MY son, in many things you must be as one ignorant, and esteem yourself

as one dead upon the earth, and to whom the whole world is crucified.

You must, too, turn a deaf ear to many things, and give your thoughts rather to the things which belong unto your peace.

It is better to turn away your eyes from such things as offend you, and to leave every one to his own opinion, rather than to be subject to angry discussions.

If you stand well with God, and keep your eye on His approval, you will very easily bear a defeat.

2. O Lord, to what a pass are we come! Behold a temporal loss is bewailed, and for a little gain we toil and run; while a spiritual loss makes little impression on our minds, and hardly ever is thought of again.

That which is of little or no value absorbs us, and that which is above all things necessary slips out of our minds; for the whole man sinks down into outward things, and unless he soon wakes up to his condition, he will willingly remain immersed in them.

CHAPTER XLV.

That we must not Trust every one, and that it is a common thing to Slip with the Tongue.

1. GRANT me help, O Lord, in trouble, for vain is the help of man.

How often have I failed to find faithfulness, where I thought myself sure of it!

How often too have I found it, where I least expected it!

Vain therefore is confidence in man, but the salvation of the righteous is in Thee, O God.

Blessed be Thou, O Lord my God, in all things which happen to us.

We are weak and unstable, we are easily deceived and change.

2. Who is the man who is able so cautiously and so circumspectly at all times to watch over himself, as not sometimes to fall into some deception or perplexity?

But he who trusts in Thee, O Lord, and seeks Thee with simplicity of heart, does not so easily slip.

And if he does fall into some tribulation, however much involved he may be, he will more quickly be delivered out of it by Thee, or comforted by Thee, for Thou wilt not forsake, even unto the end, him who trusts in Thee.

A faithful friend is but seldom found, who abides steadfast through all his friend's troubles.

Thou, O Lord, Thou alone art most faithful at all times, and besides Thee there is none else.

3. O how truly wise was that holy soul who said, "My mind is firmly settled and grounded in Christ."

If it were so with me, then the fear of man would not be felt by me, nor the darts of words move me.

Who can foresee all things? who can provide against future evils?

If events, even when foreseen, often hurt us, how can those which are unforeseen do otherwise than fall upon us heavily?

But why did I, wretched creature, not exercise more foresight? why also did I so readily trust others?

But we are men, nothing else but frail men, though by many we may be reckoned and called angels.

Whom shall I trust, O Lord, whom shall I trust but Thee?

Thou art the Truth, which neither can deceive, nor be deceived.

And, on the other hand, 'every man is a liar,' weak, fickle, and fallible, especially in speech;

so that scarcely should that be at once credited which bears upon the face of it the appearance of truth.

4. O how wisely hast Thou warned us to beware of men; and because a man's foes are those of his own household, we must not believe it, if any one should say 'Lo here, or lo there!'

I have learnt it to my cost, and O that this bitter experience may render me more cautious, and not more foolish.

'Be guarded,' says a certain one, 'be guarded, and do not repeat what I say;' and whilst I am silent about it, and think he is keeping it secret, he tells it himself, who had forbidden me to do so; and thus, having immediately betrayed both me and himself, he goes his way.

From such prattlers and careless men protect me, O Lord, lest I fall into their hands, or follow their bad example.

Give to my lips truth and firmness, and remove far from me a deceitful tongue.

What I do not like to bear from others, I ought myself in every way to avoid.

5. O what a good thing it is, and what peace it brings, not to talk about others, and not to believe all that is said without inquiry, nor to give it currency; to lay one's self open only to a few, and always to seek after Thee, the Searcher of the heart.

Nor should we be carried away with every wind of words, but we should be guided by the desire of doing all our actions, inward and outward, according to the good pleasure of Thy Will.

How safe it is for the preservation of heavenly grace, to avoid the notice of men, and not to wish for what wins the admiration of the world; but to pursue with the utmost care what tends to amendment of life and fervour.

How many have been injured through their virtue having become known and specially praised!

How healthily has grace grown up, when unnoticed in this fragile life — a life entirely made up of temptation and conflict!

CHAPTER XLVI.

Of Confidence in God when Words are darted at us.

1. MY son, stand firmly, and trust in Me; for what are words but words? They fly through the air, but hurt not a stone.

If you are in fault, consider that you should gladly wish to correct yourself; but if your conscience does not reprove you, reflect that you should be ready cheerfully to suffer this for God's sake.

It is little enough to have to bear sometimes a few words, when you cannot yet take well hard blows.

And why do such small things go to your heart, if it is not that you are yet carnal and care more for human opinion than you should?

For because you shrink from being despised, and do not like to be reproved for your faults, you try to shelter yourself under excuses.

2. But search into yourself a little more deeply, and you will find that the world, and the vain love of pleasing men, are still alive in your heart.

For when you shun being trodden under foot and put to shame for your faults, it is manifest that you are neither truly humble, nor truly dead to the world, nor the world crucified to you.

But regard My words, and you will not care for ten thousand words of men.

Behold, if all, which with the bitterest malice they could invent, should be said against you, what hurt would it do you, if you suffered it to pass entirely away, and did not care a straw about it?

Could they pluck even one hair out of your head?

3. But those who do not lead an inward life,

and have not God before their eyes, are easily disturbed by a word of blame.

But he who trusts in Me, and does not desire to stand in his own judgment, shall be free from the fear of men.

For I am the Judge and the Discerner of the secrets of all hearts; I know how the matter stands; I know who is the injurer, and who is the injured.

From Me that word proceeded, it happened, that is, by My permission, that the thoughts of many hearts may be revealed.

I shall judge the guilty and the innocent, but I willed to try them both beforehand by a secret judgment.

4. The testimony of men is often erroneous: but My judgment is true; it shall stand and not be overthrown.

It is for the most part hidden, and to few is made known as to individual cases; yet it never errs, nor can err, although to the eyes of the foolish it may not seem right.

In every thing which you have to decide, you must, therefore, have recourse to Me, and not rely upon your own judgment.

For the just man will not be disturbed, whatever may happen to him from God; and if an unjust charge be laid against him, he will not be much concerned about it.

But neither will he allow a vain feeling of exultation, if by others he is justly vindicated.

For he considers that I am He Who "searcheth the reins and heart," and judgeth not according to the face and human appearance.

For often that which according to human opinion is a subject of praise, is in My sight worthy of blame.

5. O Lord God, Just Judge, Strong and Patient, Thou Who knowest the frailty and depravity of men, be Thou my strength and all my confidence, for my own conscience does not suffice me.

Thou knowest what I do not know, and therefore I ought to accept humbly every reproof, and to bear it with meekness.

Pardon me, therefore, and be merciful to me as often as I have acted otherwise, and grant me the next time the grace of greater endurance.

For it is better for me to trust in Thy abundant mercy for pardon, than to set the righteousness which I imagine in myself against the misgivings of the lurking-places of my conscience.

Although I may be conscious to myself of no sin, yet am I not on that account justified, for without Thy mercy 'in Thy sight shall no man living be justified.'

CHAPTER XLVII.

That all Things, however grievous, are to be borne for the sake of Eternal Life.

1. MY son, let not the labours you have undertaken for My sake break you down, neither let trials make you continually gloomy; but let My promise give you strength and solace in every thing that befalls you.

I am able to reward you, above all measure and degree.

You will not have to bear this long, nor always to be weighed down with troubles.

Wait a little while, and you shall see the speedy end of your evils.

The hour will come when there shall be an end of all toil and tumult.

Poor and brief is all that passes away with time.

2. Do what you have to do, work faithfully in My vineyard; I will be thy Reward.

Write, read, sing, mourn, be silent, pray, bear opposition manfully; eternal life is worth all these conflicts, and greater than these.

There shall come peace in one day, which is known to the Lord. There shall not then be day nor night as now, but unchanging light, infinite brightness, unbroken peace, and secure rest.

You shall not say then, 'Who shall deliver me from the body of this death?' neither shall you cry 'Woe is me, that my sojourning is prolonged;' for death shall be swallowed up in victory, and health shall be unfailing, and there shall be no more anxiety, but blessed joy, and sweet and lovely companionship.

3. O, if you had seen the everlasting crowns of the Saints in Heaven, and with what glory they now rejoice, who were by this world once counted contemptible, and in a manner unworthy of life itself, you would indeed at once humble yourself to the dust, and would wish rather to be under all than to be over any one; neither would you desire the days of this life to be pleasant, but you would joyfully prefer to suffer tribulation for God's sake, and would consider it the greatest gain to be reckoned as nothing amongst men.

4. O if you could have a taste for these things, and let them sink deeply into your heart, how would you dare even once to complain?

Is it not for the sake of eternal life that all these pains are to be borne?

It is no small matter, to gain or to lose the Kingdom of God.

Lift up, therefore, your face unto Heaven;

behold, I and all My Saints with Me, who had in this world a sharp conflict, now rejoice, now are comforted, now are in safety, now are at rest; and they shall remain with Me in My Father's Kingdom for ever.

CHAPTER XLVIII.

On the Day of Eternity, and this Life's Distresses.

1. O MOST blessed mansion of the City which is above!

O most bright day of eternity, which night does not darken, but which the highest Truth perpetually illuminates.

Day, ever joyful, ever secure, ever changeless!

O that that day would come, and that all these temporal things would have an end!

It shines indeed to the Saints with a bright and unceasing radiance, but to us wayfarers upon earth it is seen afar off as through a glass.

2. The heavenly inhabitants know how joyful that day is; the exiled sons of Eve know to their grief how bitter and wearisome this life is.

The days of this life are few and evil, full of sorrow and care.

Here a man is defiled by many sins, ensnared by many passions, restrained by many fears, racked by many cares, distracted by many interests, entangled by many vanities, encompassed by many errors, worn out by many labours, weighed down by many temptations, weakened by pleasures, and tortured by cravings.

3. O when will there be an end of all these evils?

When shall I be delivered from the miserable bondage of evil passions? when shall I be mindful, O Lord, of Thee alone? when shall I fully rejoice in Thee? when shall I enjoy true freedom without any obstacle, without any trouble of mind or body?

When will there be solid peace—peace unbroken and secure, peace within and without, peace on all sides steadfast?

O good Jesu, when shall I stand to behold Thee?

When shall I contemplate the glory of Thy Kingdom?

When wilt Thou be all in all to me?

O when shall I be with Thee in Thy Kingdom, which from eternity Thou hast prepared for them that love Thee?

I am left poor, and as an exile in a hostile country, where wars happen daily and the greatest misfortunes.

4. Console me in my banishment, soothe my sorrow; for all my desires and aspirations are towards Thee.

For whatever consolation this world offers is but a burden to me.

I long to enjoy intimate communion with Thee, but am unable to attain to it.

I desire to cleave to heavenly things, but temporal things and my unmortified passions press me down.

With my mind I desire to rise above all these things, but with my flesh I am against my higher will drawn under their power.

Thus I—unhappy man—am at war against myself, and am wearisome to myself; whilst my spirit draws me up, my flesh tries to drag me down.

5. O what do I inwardly suffer, whilst with my mind I am occupied with heavenly objects, lo, presently a crowd of carnal thoughts and temptations interrupts my prayer!

'My God, be not Thou far from me, nor turn Thy Face away from Thy servant in displeasure.'

Cast forth Thy lightning and scatter them; send out Thine arrows, and let all the phantoms of the enemy be dispelled.

Gather up all my senses unto Thee; make me forgetful of worldly things, grant me instantly to put away with scorn all vicious imaginations.

Strengthen me, Eternal Truth, that no vanity may be able to affect me.

Come to me, O Thou Sweetness Celestial, and let all impurity flee before Thy Face.

Pardon me also, and mercifully look upon me, as often as I wander from Thee in my prayer.

For I must truly confess, that I am accustomed to be very distracted.

For I am very often not there where in body I am standing or sitting, but I am rather there where my thoughts have borne me.

Where my thoughts are, there am I; where my thoughts habitually are, there is that which I love.

That readily occurs to me, which naturally delights me, or by habit is pleasing.

6. Wherefore Thou, O Eternal Truth, hast plainly said, 'Where thy treasure is, there will thy heart be also.'

If I love Heaven, my thoughts will run on heavenly things.

If I love the world, I shall rejoice about temporal happiness and find sorrow in temporal adversity.

If I love the flesh, I shall very often dwell upon the things of the flesh.

If I love the spirit, I shall find pleasure in thinking on spiritual things.

For whatever I love, I delight to speak of and to hear of, and I carry home with me the impressions of those things.

But blessed is the man, who for Thy sake, O Lord, foregoes all created things, who does violence to his nature and crucifies the lusts of the flesh by fervour of the spirit; so that, with a tranquil conscience, he may offer pure prayer to Thee, and be worthy to mix with the angelic choirs—all earthly things for the time being inwardly and outwardly put away.

CHAPTER XLIX.

Of the Desire of Eternal Life, and how great are the Rewards which are promised to those who strive for them.

1. MY son, when you feel the desire of eternal bliss to be shed down upon you from above, and you experience a longing to depart out of the tabernacle of the body, that you may be able to contemplate My glory without shadow of change, expand your soul, and drink in with eagerness this holy inspiration.

Render most abundant thanks to the Heavenly Goodness, which treats you so graciously—visiting you mercifully, enkindling you fervently, sustaining you powerfully, lest by your own tendency you sink down to the things of earth.

For it is not by your own thoughtfulness or effort you receive this, but simply through the condescension of heavenly grace and the Divine regard; in order that you may grow in virtues, and advance in humility, and be prepared for future conflicts, learn to cleave to Me with the whole affection of your heart, and to serve Me with a fervent will.

2. My son, the fire often burns, but without smoke the flame does not ascend.

So also the desires of some turn towards heavenly things, and yet they are not free from the temptation of carnal affection.

They do not, therefore, act purely for the honour of God, when they make requests so earnestly to Him.

Such also are oftentimes your desires, when they seem to be most earnest; for those are not pure and perfect desires, which have the stain of self-seeking upon them.

3. Do not seek what is pleasant and profitable to yourself, but what is acceptable to Me and honours Me; for if you judged rightly, you would prefer to follow My appointment rather than your own desire, or any thing that is to be desired.

I know your desire, and have heard your frequent groanings.

Now you wish to enjoy the glorious liberty of the sons of God; now the eternal habitation, the Heavenly Country with its fulness of joy delights you.

But that hour is not yet come; for now it is a different time—a time of conflict, a time of labour and of trial.

You long to be filled with the Sovereign Good, but as yet you cannot attain to it.

I am He, wait for Me, saith the Lord, until the Kingdom of God shall come.

4. You are still to be tried on earth, and in manifold ways to be exercised.

Sometimes you shall receive consolation, but an abundant satisfaction shall not be granted you.

Therefore be strong and courageous, as well in doing as in suffering things from which nature shrinks.

You must put on the new man, and be changed yourself into another man.

You ought often to do what you do not wish, and what you do wish you ought to leave undone.

What you do for others shall have success, what you undertake to please yourself shall fail.

What others say shall be listened to; what you say shall be regarded as of no importance; others shall ask and receive, and you shall ask and be refused.

5. Others shall be spoken of as great men, but concerning you they shall not say a word.

Others shall have charge of this or that, but you shall be considered as fit for nothing.

Nature will sometimes feel sad at this, but if you bear it silently you will reap much fruit.

In these and in many similar things the faithful servant of the Lord is wont to be tried, how far he is seeking to deny himself in all things, and to break entirely his own will.

There is scarcely any thing in which you stand so much in need of dying to yourself, as in seeing and suffering the things which are contrary to your own will; and most of all, when that is commanded to be done, which in your own judgment seems unsuitable and useless.

And because, being under authority, you do not dare to resist the higher power, therefore it seems to you hard to walk according to the will of another, and to have to leave your own will entirely.

6. But, think, my son, of the fruit of your labours, of their speedy end, and the exceeding great reward; and you will no longer find anything burdensome, but have a very strong consolation in your suffering.

For in exchange for the trifling exercise of your will, which you now freely forsake, you shall for ever have your own will in heaven.

For there you will find every thing as you wish, and all that you can desire.

There all good shall be within your power, and there shall be no fear of losing it.

There your will and My will shall be alike; and you shall covet nothing out of Me, nor have any private wish.

There no one shall oppose you, no one shall complain of you, no one shall thwart you, no one shall stand in your way; but all things desirable shall be at one and the same time present, and shall satisfy all your longings, and fill them to the full.

There will I give glory for the shame which has been endured; a garment of praise for heaviness; a seat in the Kingdom for ever for the lowest place on earth.

There the fruit of obedience shall be manifested; the toil of penitence shall bring joy; and lowly subjection shall be gloriously crowned.

7. Now, therefore, bow yourself humbly under all, and do not be careful to inquire whether or not they have a right to order you; but let it be your principal concern—whether he who seeks any thing from you or suggests any thing to you be superior, equal, or inferior—to take it all in good part, and to labour with a sincere will to perform it.

Let one man seek one thing, and another another; let one man glory in this, and another in that, and receive a thousand thousand praises;

but you for your part seek nothing of the kind, but rejoice in the contempt of yourself, and in My good pleasure and honour only.

This must be your desire, that God may be always glorified whether by life or by death.

CHAPTER L.

How one in Desolation ought to resign Himself into God's Hands.

1. O LORD God, Holy Father, be Thou now and for ever blessed, because as Thou wilt, so it is come to pass, and what Thou doest is good.

Let Thy servant rejoice in Thee, not in himself, nor in any one else; for Thou art alone true gladness, Thou art my hope and my crown, Thou art my joy and my honour, O Lord.

What has Thy servant but what he has received from Thee, and without any merit of his own?

All things are Thine, which Thou hast bestowed, and which Thou hast made.

I am poor and in trouble from my youth; and my soul is sorrowful, sometimes even unto tears; and my spirit is disquieted within me, because of impending sufferings.

2. I desire the joy of peace, the peace of Thy

children I crave, whom Thou feedest in the light of Thy consolation.

If Thou give peace, if Thou infuse holy joy, the soul of Thy servant shall be full of melody, and devout in Thy praise.

But if Thou withdraw Thy presence (as Thou art very accustomed to do), Thy servant will not be able to run in the way of Thy commandments; but he will rather bend his knees, and smite his breast, because it is not as it was yesterday and the day before, when Thy candle shined upon his head, and when he was sheltered beneath the covering of Thy wings from the assaults of temptation.

3. O righteous Father, and ever to be praised, the hour has come when Thy servant is to be tried.

O beloved Father, it is meet that in this hour Thy servant should suffer something for Thy sake.

O Father, always to be adored, the hour is come, which from eternity Thou didst foresee should arrive, when for a little while Thy servant in his outer life should be oppressed, that in his inner life he might ever live before Thee; that he should be for a little while slighted, humbled, and in the sight of man fail, so that he may rise with Thee at the dawn of the new Light, and be glorified in Heaven.

O Holy Father, Thou hast so ordained it, Thou hast so willed it, and it has come to pass as Thou didst ordain.

4. For this is a favour to Thy friend, that for love of Thee he may suffer and have tribulation in this world, as often as, and from whatever source, Thou mayest permit such trials to come.

Nothing takes place on the earth without Thy counsel, and Thy providence, and Thy purpose.

It is good for me, O Lord, that Thou hast humbled me, that I may learn Thy righteous judgments, and may cast away all proud and presumptuous thoughts.

It is profitable to me that shame has covered my face, that I might seek Thy consolation, and not that of men.

I have also learnt from this to fear Thy unsearchable judgments, which fall upon the just as well as on the sinner, but not without equity and justice.

5. I give Thee thanks, that Thou hast not spared my sins, but hast bruised me with bitter stripes, inflicting pain and sending anxieties upon me both within and without.

There is not one who can console me of all that are under Heaven; none but Thyself, O Lord my God, Heavenly Physician of souls, Who woundest and healest, Who bringest down to hell and bringest back again.

Let me be under Thy discipline, and let Thy rod itself teach me.

6. Behold, beloved Father, I am in Thy hands; under Thy correcting rod I bow myself.

Strike my back and my neck, that my crookedness may be bent into conformity with Thy will.

Make me a devout and humble disciple (as Thou hast been accustomed to do me good), that my steps may henceforth be in accordance with Thy will.

To Thee I commit myself and all that is mine, to be corrected; it is better to be chastened here, than hereafter.

Thou knowest all things, and each thing in particular, and nothing in the human conscience is hidden from Thine Eye.

Thou knowest the events which are future before they come to pass, and hast no need to be informed or reminded of the things which are taking place on earth.

Thou knowest what is expedient for my progress, and how greatly trials serve to cleanse away the rust of vices.

Do with me according to the good pleasure of Thy will, and do not despise my sinful life—

to none better or more clearly known than to Thyself alone.

7. Grant me, O Lord, to know what I ought to know, to love what I ought to love, to praise what delights Thee most, to value what is precious in Thy sight, to hate what is offensive to Thee.

Do not suffer me to judge according to the sight of my eyes, nor to pass sentence according to the hearing of the ears of ignorant men; but to discern with a true judgment between things visible and spiritual, and above all things always to inquire what is the good pleasure of Thy will.

8. When men judge according to their senses, they often err; and the lovers of the world, by loving visible things only, are deceived.

For what is a man the better, for being thought greater by man?

The deceitful deceive the deceitful; the vain deceive the vain; the blind, the blind; the weak, the weak, when he extols him; and, indeed, when he is receiving empty praise he is rather being put to shame.

For a man is what he is in Thy sight, and nothing more, according to the saying of the humble Saint Francis.

CHAPTER LI.

That a Man must occupy himself with Humble Works when he is unable to attain to the things which are Highest.

1. MY son, you cannot always sustain the more ardent desires after virtue, nor abide in the higher degrees of contemplation; but you will have sometimes on account of original corruption to descend to lower things, and to bear the burden of this corruptible life, though unwillingly and wearily.

As long as you carry about with you this mortal body, you will feel weariness and heaviness of heart.

You ought, therefore, as long as you are in the flesh, often to bewail the burden of the flesh; in so far as it hinders you from spiritual exercises, and from giving yourself without intermission to divine contemplation.

2. Then it will be advantageous for you to turn to commonplace and outward occupations, and to refresh yourself by doing good actions; to wait My return and heavenly visitation with great confidence; to suffer patiently your banished state and dryness of spirit, until I shall

again visit you, and deliver you from all your anxieties.

For I will cause you to forget your toils, and thoroughly to enjoy inward peace.

I will spread out before you the pastures of the Scriptures, that with an enlarged heart you may begin to run in the way of My commandments.

And you shall say, "The sufferings of this present time are not worthy to be compared with the glory, that shall be revealed in us."

CHAPTER LII.

That a Man ought to consider himself more worthy of Chastisement than of Consolation.

1. O LORD, I am not worthy of Thy consolation, nor of any spiritual visitation; and therefore Thou dealest justly with me, when I am left poor and desolate.

For if I could shed a sea of tears, still I should not be worthy of Thy consolation.

I am not, then, worthy of any thing but to be chastised and punished; because I have frequently and grievously offended Thee, and in many things been very remiss.

Therefore, having well weighed the matter,

I come to the conclusion, that I am unworthy of the least of Thy mercies.

But Thou art gracious and merciful, and willest not that those whom Thou hast made should perish, in order to shew the riches of Thy goodness upon the vessels of mercy; and Thou dost vouchsafe to comfort Thy servant beyond all merit of his own, and all human bounds.

For Thy consolations are not like human words.

2. What have I done, O Lord, that Thou shouldest grant me any heavenly consolation?

I do not recollect that I have done any thing good, but that I have been always prone to evil, and slow to amend.

This is true, and I cannot deny it. If I were to say otherwise, Thou wouldest rise up against me, and there would be no one to defend me.

What have I deserved on account of my sins, but hell and eternal fire?

I confess with perfect truth that, as I am worthy of all ridicule and contempt, I ought not to be reckoned amongst Thy faithful servants.

And although it pains me to hear this, yet for Truth's sake I will convict myself of my sins, so that the more easily I may gain Thy pity.

3. What shall I—guilty and covered with shame—say? I have no mouth for speaking,

except it be this one word—'I have sinned, O Lord, I have sinned; have mercy upon me, pardon me.'

Spare me a little, that I may mourn over my sins, before I depart into the land of darkness and of the shadow of death.

What dost Thou so much require of a guilty and miserable sinner, as that he should be contrite, and should humble himself for his sins?

From true contrition and a humbled heart springs hope of pardon; the troubled conscience is reconciled; lost grace is recovered; man is sheltered from the wrath to come, and God and the repentant soul meet together with a holy kiss.

4. Humble contrition for sins is a sacrifice acceptable to Thee, O Lord, a savour far sweeter in Thy sight than fumes of incense.

This is also the fragrant ointment, which Thou didst desire to be poured upon Thy sacred feet; for a contrite and humble heart Thou never didst despise.

Here is the place of refuge from the angry face of the Enemy; here whatever pollution may have been contracted elsewhere, is purified and washed away.

CHAPTER LIII.

That the Grace of God does not mingle with the Worldly-minded.

1. MY son, My grace is precious, and does not admit of being blended with external things and worldly consolations.

Therefore you must cast away all hindrances to grace, if you desire that it should be poured forth within you.

Seek privacy; love to dwell alone with yourself; seek not for conversation with any one, but rather pour out devout prayer to God, that you may keep your heart contrite and your conscience pure.

Esteem the whole world as nothing; prefer the service of God before all outward things.

For you cannot equally serve Me and delight in transitory things.

You ought to keep aloof from acquaintances and friends, and deprive yourself of all temporal comfort.

So the blessed Apostle Peter exhorts the faithful Christians to keep themselves 'as strangers and pilgrims' in this world.

2. O what confidence would the dying man have, who felt that he was not detained in this world by attachment to any thing!

But the mind as yet feeble is unable to grasp the thought of such an entire separation from all things, nor can the carnal man know the liberty of the spiritual man.

But if he sincerely wishes to become spiritual, he must begin to break off from those who are far off, and from those who are near, and to beware of no one more than of himself.

If you perfectly conquer yourself, you will the more easily subdue all things else.

For the perfect victory is the victory over self; for he who keeps himself in subjection, having his sensual appetites in subordination to his reason, and his reason in all things obedient to Me, he is a true conqueror of himself, and lord of the world.

3. If you ardently long to scan the height, you must start vigorously, and put the axe to the root; so that you may tear out and destroy every subtle and inordinate tendency to self-love, exclusiveness, and aggrandisement.

For this vice—a man's inordinate love of himself—is at the bottom of almost every thing which has to be thoroughly overcome; when this evil is overcome and driven out, then there will be great peace, and immediate tranquillity.

But because few labour to become perfectly dead to self, and to keep self entirely out of their thoughts, therefore they continue in a state of embarrassment, and are unable to rise in spirit above themselves.

But he who desires to walk freely with Me, must mortify all depraved and inordinate affections, and not eagerly cling to any creature through self-love.

CHAPTER LIV.

Of the Different Motions of Nature and Grace.

1. MY son, carefully observe the motions of Nature and of Grace; for they move in a very contrary yet subtle manner, and with difficulty are they distinguished even by a spiritual and inwardly enlightened man.

All men indeed desire good, and pretend to something good in what they say or do, therefore under the semblance of good many are deceived.

2. Nature is crafty and seduces many, ensnares and dupes them, and has always herself for her end.

But Grace walks in simplicity, and abstains from all appearance of evil, makes no false pretences, and does all things purely for God, in Whom also she finally reposes.

3. Nature is loth to die, reluctant to be kept

down or overcome, or to be under, and objects to be in a state of subjection.

But Grace is eager for self-mortification, resists sensuality, seeks to be in subjection, desires to be defeated, does not wish to use her own liberty, loves to be kept under discipline, and has no desire to be over any one, but desires always to live, and remain, and be under God, and for God's sake is ready humbly to bow down to every human creature.

4. Nature labours for her own advantage, and considers how much she may get from another.

But Grace does not seek her own advantage and comfort, but rather what may be for the good of many.

5. Nature is fond of receiving honour and respect.

But Grace faithfully ascribes all honour and glory to God.

6. Nature dreads shame and contempt.

But Grace rejoices to suffer reproach for the Name of Jesus.

7. Nature loves ease and bodily rest.

But Grace cannot be idle, but gladly undergoes toil.

8. Nature likes to have things different from others and fine, and shuns what is mean and coarse.

But Grace delights in what is plain and

humble, does not spurn what is rough, nor refuses to be clothed in rags.

9. Nature respects temporal things, rejoices at earthly gains, grieves at losses, resents the slightest injurious word.

But Grace looks to things eternal, does not cling to temporal things, is not disturbed by losses, is not provoked by harsh words; because she places her treasure and her joy in Heaven, where nothing perishes.

10. Nature is covetous, and more ready to receive than to give, and loves to have and to keep things to herself.

But Grace is kind and ready to share with others, shuns what is singular, is content with a little, thinks it more blessed to give than to receive.

11. Nature leans towards creatures, to her own flesh, to vanity, and to running about.

But Grace draws the soul towards God, and to virtues, renounces creatures, shuns the world, hates the desires of the flesh, restrains wanderings about, and blushes to appear in public.

12. Nature delights to have some outward comfort, which brings gratification of sense.

But Grace seeks to be comforted by God alone, and delights in the Supreme Good above all visible things.

13. Nature does every thing for gain, and for

her own convenience, can do nothing unless she is paid for it, but hopes to get either an equivalent or an advantage in exchange for every kindness, or else praise or favour; and she desires that her deeds, gifts, and words should be highly estimated.

But Grace seeks nothing temporal, nor asks for any other prize than God alone for her reward, nor does she desire temporal things beyond what is necessary, except it be that she might employ them for the obtaining of things eternal.

14. Nature is fond of having many friends and relations, boasts of station and of birth, makes a point of pleasing those in power, fawns on the rich, praises those who are similar to herself.

But Grace loves even enemies, is not puffed up by a crowd of friends, makes no account of place or birth, unless it is accompanied with greater virtue; she favours the poor rather than the rich, sympathizes more with the innocent than with the powerful, rejoices in the truth and not in deceit, ever exhorts the good to 'covet earnestly the best gifts,' and through virtues to grow like to the Son of God.

15. Nature soon complains of any lack or inconvenience.

Grace bears want with constancy.

16. Nature refers every thing to herself, contends for self, and asserts herself.

But Grace refers all to God, from Whom all things originally came; she ascribes no good thing to herself, does not arrogantly presume, nor contend, nor prefer her own opinion to that of others, but in every feeling and opinion submits herself to the Eternal Wisdom and the Divine Judgment.

17. Nature is anxious to know secrets and to hear news, wishes to appear abroad, to test things by experience, desires to be known, and to do something from which may arise praise and admiration.

But Grace does not care to learn what is new or curious—because all this springs from the old corruption, since there is nothing new or lasting upon earth.

Therefore Grace teaches to guard the senses, to avoid vain complacency and ostentation, humbly to hide things deserving praise and admiration, and in every thing and in all knowledge to seek the profit of others, and the praise and glory of God.

She does not wish herself nor her effects to be publicly praised, but that God, Who bestows all things out of pure love, should be blessed for all His gifts.

18. This grace is a supernatural light, and a

certain special gift of God, a seal of His elect, a pledge of everlasting salvation, which draws up a man from the love of earth to the love of heaven, and renders him spiritual instead of carnal.

Therefore the more nature is held down and overcome, so much the more will grace be poured into the soul; and every day by fresh visitations the inner man will become reformed after the image of God.

CHAPTER LV.

On the Corruption of Nature, and the Efficacy of Divine Grace.

1. O LORD my God, Who hast created me after Thine own image and likeness, grant me this Grace, which Thou hast shewed me to be so great and so necessary to salvation; that I may overcome this corrupt nature of mine, which draws me to sin and to perdition.

For I feel in my flesh the law of sin warring against the law of my mind, and leading me captive to obey in many things the sensual appetite; neither can I resist its passions, unless Thy most holy grace, ardently infused into my heart, assist me.

2. There is need of Thy grace, and of great

grace, that I may overcome my nature, which always was prone to evil from my youth.

For through the first man, Adam, Nature fell and was corrupted by sin, and the penalty of this stain has descended unto all mankind, so that "Nature" itself—which was made upright and good by Thee—is the term we now use for the evil desires and the weakness of corrupt nature; in that now, when it is left to itself, its promptings tend towards wickedness and to lower things.

For the little strength which remains is, as it were, a spark smouldering in the embers.

This is natural reason itself, enveloped with much darkness, yet still possessing a power of distinguishing between good and evil, between true and false; although it is unable to fulfil all that it approves, and no longer retains the full light of truth, nor healthfulness of the affections.

3. Hence it is, my God, that I delight in Thy law after the inward man, knowing that Thy commandment is good, just, and holy, and that it reproves every thing that is wrong and sinful—which ought to be avoided.

But with the flesh I serve the law of sin, when I obey sensual desire rather than reason.

Hence it is that 'to will is present with me; but how to perform that which is good I find not.'

Hence it is that I often make many good

resolutions, but because grace is needed to help my infirmity, at a slight resistance I fall back and fail.

Hence it happens, that I know the way of perfection, and see clearly what I ought to do; but, weighed down by my own corruption, I do not rise to higher things.

4. O Lord, how very necessary Thy grace is to me, to begin, to go on with, and to complete any thing good.

For without it I can do nothing, but in Thee I can do all things—Thy grace strengthening me.

O truly celestial grace! without which our merits are nothing, and our gifts of nature not to be esteemed.

No arts, no riches, no beauty or strength, no ability or eloquence, are of any value before Thee, O Lord, without Thy grace.

For gifts of nature are common to good and bad, but grace or love is the peculiar gift of Thine elect, and they that bear this mark are accounted worthy of eternal life.

This grace is so excellent, that neither the gift of prophecy, nor the working of miracles, nor the understanding of deep mysteries, is of any worth without it.

But neither faith, nor hope, nor any other virtue, is acceptable to Thee without charity and grace.

5. O most blessed grace, which makest the poor in spirit, rich in virtues; and makest the rich in many goods, humble in heart!

Come Thou, descend upon me, refresh me early with Thy mercy and Thy consolation, that my soul may not faint for weariness and dryness of spirit.

I beseech Thee, O Lord, that I may find grace in Thy sight, for Thy grace is sufficient for me, though the things which nature desires be wanting.

If I am harassed and tempted by many tribulations, I will fear no evil, so long as Thy grace is with me.

She is my strength, and brings counsel and help.

She is more powerful than all enemies, and more wise than all counsellors.

6. She is the mistress of truth, the teacher of discipline, the light of the heart, the solace of the oppressed, the banisher of sadness, the expeller of fear, the nurse of devotion, and the source of tears.

What am I without her but a dry tree and an unprofitable branch, such as would be cast away?

Let Thy grace, therefore, O Lord, always prevent and follow me, and make me to be continually given to good works, through Jesus Christ, Thy Son. Amen.

CHAPTER LVI.

That we ought to Deny Ourselves, and to Imitate Christ by the Cross.

1. MY son, as much as you can go out of yourself, so much will you be able to enter into Me.

As the absence of all craving for outward things brings inward peace, so the setting aside of self inwardly unites you to God.

I wish you to learn perfect renunciation of yourself to My will, without opposition or complaint.

Follow Me; 'I am the Way, the Truth, and the Life.'

Without the Way, you cannot go; without the Truth, you cannot know; without the Life, you cannot live.

I am the Way, which you ought to follow; the Truth, which you ought to believe; the Life, which you ought to hope for.

I am the Way, unchangeable; the Truth, infallible; the Life, endless.

I am the Way which is straightest, the Sovereign Truth, the true Life, the blessed Life, the Life uncreated.

If you abide in My way you shall know the

truth, and the truth shall make you free, and you shall lay hold of eternal life.

2. If you desire to enter into life, keep the commandments.

If you desire to know the truth, believe Me.

If you desire to be perfect, sell all.

If you wish to be My disciple, deny yourself.

If you wish to obtain the blessed life, despise this present life.

If you desire to be exalted in Heaven, humble yourself in this world.

If you will to reign with Me, bear the Cross with Me.

For only the servants of the Cross find the life of Blessedness and of true light.

3. O Lord Jesus, since Thy life was strict and despised by the world, grant me grace to follow Thy steps, and share with Thee the contempt of the world.

For the servant is not greater than his Lord, nor the disciple above his master.

Let Thy servant be trained after Thy life, for in it is my safety and true holiness.

Whatever else I hear and read does not refresh me, nor give me full delight.

4. My son, since you know these things, and read them all, blessed shall you be if you do them.

' He that hath My commandments and keepeth them, he it is that loveth Me; and I will love him, and will manifest Myself unto him,' and will make him sit together with Me in My Father's Kingdom.

Therefore, O Lord Jesus, as Thou hast said and promised, so may it happen unto me, and may I deserve it.

I have received, I have received from Thy hand the cross; I will bear it, I will bear it even unto death, as Thou hast laid it upon me.

Truly the life of a good Religious man is a cross, but it leads to Paradise.

We have begun; we may not go back, neither is it right to leave it.

5. Onward, brethren, onward let us go together! Jesus will be with us.

For the sake of Jesus we have taken up this cross; for the sake of Jesus let us continue to bear it.

He will be our Helper, Who is our Guide and Forerunner.

Behold our King marches before us, Who will fight for us.

Let us follow Him bravely, let no one shrink from fear; let us be prepared to die valiantly in battle, and let us not bring disgrace on our glory by turning back from the Cross.

CHAPTER LVII.

That a Man should not be too Dejected at Failures or Trial.

1. MY son, patience and humility in adversity are more pleasing to Me, than much consolation and devotion in prosperity.

Why are you so grieved by every little thing which is said against you?

If it had been much greater, you ought not to have been troubled at it.

But now dismiss it from your thoughts; it is not the first trial, nor any thing new, neither will it be the last, if you continue to live.

You are brave enough, when no trial comes against you; you can give good advice, and know how to strengthen others by your words, but when sudden tribulation is at your door, you fail in counsel and in courage.

2. Consider then your great frailty, which you have very often experienced on slight occasions, yet for your salvation these occur.

When these and similar things happen, put them out of your thoughts as much as possible; and, if tribulation have touched you, be not depressed nor much perplexed.

At least bear it patiently, if you cannot bear it joyfully.

Although it is painful to you to hear it, and you feel indignant, yet restrain yourself, and do not suffer any improper word to go forth from your lips whereby the weak may be offended.

Soon shall the angry feelings which are stirred up subside, and the pain of the soul be sweetly soothed by returning grace.

I still live, saith the Lord, and am ready to help you, and to impart more than ordinary comfort, if you put your trust in Me and earnestly call upon Me.

3. Be more calm, and gird yourself to greater endurance.

All is not lost, because you feel yourself very often tried or much tempted.

You are man, and not God; you are flesh, and not an Angel.

How can you expect always to remain in the same degree of virtue, when an Angel in Heaven, and the first man in Paradise, failed to do so?

I am He Who lifts up 'those who mourn' 'to safety;' and those who recognise their own weakness, I call to the participation of My Divinity.

4. O Lord, blessed be Thy word, sweeter to my mouth than honey and the honeycomb.

What should I do in so many of my trials

and distresses, unless Thou didst comfort me by Thy holy word?

Provided that at last I reach the haven of salvation, what does it matter how much I suffer, or what I suffer?

Grant me a good end, and grant me a happy passage out of this world.

Remember me, My God, and direct me in the right way into Thy Kingdom. Amen.

CHAPTER LVIII.

That Things beyond our reach, and the Secret Judgments of God, are not to be Scrutinized.

1. MY son, avoid disputes about abstruse matters, and the mysterious judgments of God—why this man is forsaken, and that man raised to so much grace; why also one should be so much afflicted, and another so highly exalted.

· These things are beyond the reach of the human intellect, neither can any reasoning or argument unravel the mystery of the Divine judgments.

When therefore the Enemy suggests such questions to you, or if any men who are fond of subtleties enter upon these matters, reply to them in the words of the prophet,—

'Righteous art Thou, O Lord, and upright are Thy judgments.' And again—'The judgments of the Lord are true and righteous altogether.'

My judgments are to be feared, not to be discussed; the mind of man cannot comprehend them.

2. Also do not inquire nor argue about the relative merits of Saints, as to who is holier or greater than another in the Kingdom of Heaven.

Such questions often produce strife and useless disputes, and cherish a spirit of pride and vainglory, whereby envy and dissension arise; whilst one proudly strives to exalt one Saint; another, another.

But the desire to know and investigate such subjects is fruitless, and is rather displeasing to the Saints themselves; for I am not the God of dissension, but of peace, which peace consists rather in genuine lowliness than in exaltation of self.

3. Some are drawn by a special devotion towards those Saints, some towards these have a greater regard; but there is often much that is human rather than divine in this.

I am He Who formed all the Saints; I gave them grace, I offered them glory.

I know the merits of each; I prevented them with the blessings of My sweetness.

I foreknew My beloved ones before the world was; I have chosen them out of the world; they did not first choose Me.

I have called them by My grace; I have drawn them by My mercy; I have brought them through various temptations.

I have poured into them vast consolations; I have given them perseverance; I have crowned their patience.

4. I know the first and the last; I embrace all with inestimable love.

I am to be praised in all My Saints; I am to be blessed and honoured above all, and in each one of those whom I have so gloriously magnified, and predestinated, without any antecedent merits of their own.

Therefore he who despises one of the least of these, does not honour the great, for I have made the small and the great.

He who disparages any of the Saints, disparages Me, and all the other Saints who are in the Kingdom of Heaven.

They are all one through the bond of charity; they have all one mind, one will, and one heart of love towards each other.

5. But still, which is of more importance, they love Me more than themselves and their own merits.

For rapt above themselves, and drawn from all

love of self, they become wholly absorbed in My love, and in it repose with delight.

Nothing is there which can turn them aside, or drag them down; for they, who are full of eternal truth, glow with the flame of an unquenchable love.

Therefore let carnal and unspiritual men, who can love nothing but selfish gratifications, cease to dispute about the state of the Saints. Such men add and take away as it pleases them, and not as it pleases eternal Truth.

6. By many it is done ignorantly, chiefly by those that are but little enlightened, and seldom able to love any thing with a purely spiritual love.

They are very much drawn by natural affection and human friendship either to these or to those; and their feelings with respect to earthly objects, they transfer to heavenly beings.

But there is an immeasurable distance between the thoughts of imperfect man himself, and those of man when enlightened by Revelation and the contemplation of things above.

7. Beware, therefore, my son, of inquiring into things too curiously which exceed your capacity; but rather make it your business and aim, that you may be found, if it be but the least, in the Kingdom of God.

And if any one did know, who was the holier

or greater in the Kingdom of Heaven, what would this knowledge profit him, unless on account of it he grew more humble in My sight, and was stirred up to a greater praise of My Name?

Much more acceptable to God does he become, who thinks about the greatness of his sins, and of his backwardness in virtues, and of how far he falls short of the perfectness of the Saints, than he who argues about which is the greater of the Saints, and which the less.

With regard to the Saints, it is better to seek their prayers with devotion and tears, and with a humble mind to implore their glorious assistance, than with vain curiosity to inquire into secrets about them.

8. They are well, quite well, contented, if men would rest contented, and cease from their vain discussions.

They do not boast of their own merits, for they ascribe nothing good to themselves, but all to Me, since I gave them all they possess out of My infinite love.

They are so filled with the love of the Divine Nature, and so overflowing with joy, that there is no glory nor happiness that is, or can be, wanting to them.

All the Saints, the higher they are in glory, the more humble they are in themselves, and the nearer and dearer to Me.

And therefore Thou hast it written—'that they did cast their crowns before God, and fell down on their faces before the Lamb, and adored Him that liveth for ever and ever.'

9. Many seek to know who is the greatest in the Kingdom of God, who know not whether they are worthy to be reckoned with the least.

It is a great thing to be even the least in Heaven, where all are great; because all shall be called, and shall be, the Sons of God.

'The least shall be as a thousand,' and 'the sinner of an hundred years shall die.'

For when the disciples asked who should be greatest in the Kingdom of Heaven, they received this answer:—

'Except ye be converted, and become as little children, ye shall not enter into the Kingdom of Heaven; whosoever therefore shall humble himself as this little child, the same is greatest in the Kingdom of Heaven.'

10. Woe to those who disdain to humble themselves, and to become as little children; for the gate of the Heavenly Kingdom will be too low for them to enter in.

Woe also to the rich, who have their consolations here, for whilst the poor are entering into the Kingdom of God, they will stand outside, wailing!

Rejoice, ye humble; and exult, ye poor, for

yours is the Kingdom of God, that is, if ye walk in truth.

CHAPTER LIX.

That all Hope and Trust is to be fixed in God alone.

1. O LORD, what is my hope which I have in this life, or what is my greatest comfort which I have from all visible things under heaven?

Is it not Thou Thyself, O Lord my God, whose mercies are without number?

When was it ever well with me without Thee? or when could it be ever ill with me, when Thou wert present?

I would rather be poor for Thee, than rich without Thee.

I would choose rather to be a pilgrim on earth with Thee, than to possess Heaven without Thee.

Where Thou art, there is Heaven; and where Thou art not, there is death and Hell.

Thou art my desire; and therefore I must sigh and cry after Thee, and call earnestly upon Thee.

In short there is none whom I can fully trust in, to bring me the help which I need in my times of trial, but Thou alone, my God.

Thou art my hope, my confidence, and my comforter; and most faithful art Thou in all things.

2. All seek their own advantage: Thou aimest at my salvation and my advancement only, and turnest all things to my profit.

And if I am exposed by Thee to various temptations and trials, all are appointed for my good, for Thou in a thousand ways art wont to prove Thy beloved servants.

In which trials Thou oughtest no less to be loved and praised, than if Thou didst fill me with heavenly consolations.

3. In Thee, therefore, O Lord my God, I place my whole trust and refuge; on Thee I cast all my tribulation and distress, for I find every thing weak and unstable, which I behold out of Thee.

For neither do a number of friends profit us, nor can strong helpers assist, nor prudent advisers give useful counsel, nor books of learned men console, nor any precious substance redeem, nor any place, however secret, defend, unless Thou Thyself assist, help, strengthen, comfort, instruct, and guard us.

4. For all the things which seem calculated to bring peace and happiness, without Thee are nothing, and bring no true happiness at all.

Thou, therefore, art the end of all good, the

highest life, the deepest wisdom that can be uttered; and to trust in Thee above all, is the strongest comfort of all Thy servants.

To Thee do I look up; in Thee do I trust, my God, Father of mercies!

Bless and sanctify my soul with Heavenly blessing, that it may become Thy holy habitation, and the seat of Thy eternal glory; and let nothing be found where Thou deignest to dwell, that may offend the eyes of Thy Majesty.

According to the multitude of Thy mercies and the greatness of Thy goodness look upon me; and hear the prayer of Thy poor servant—exiled far away in the region of the shadow of death.

Defend and preserve the soul of Thine unworthy servant amid the many risks of this corruptible life; and, by Thy grace accompanying me, direct me along the path of peace to the Country of never-failing joy and brightness. Amen.

BOOK IV.

Of Devout Exhortation to the Holy Communion.

THE VOICE OF CHRIST.

'Come unto Me all ye that labour and are heavy laden, and I will refresh you,' saith the Lord.

'The bread which I will give is My flesh—for the life of the world.'

'Take ye and eat; this is My Body which is given for you: do this in remembrance of Me.'

'He that eateth My Flesh and drinketh My Blood, dwelleth in Me, and I in him.'

'The words which I have spoken unto you are Spirit and Life.'

CHAPTER I.

With how great Reverence Christ ought to be Received.

1. THESE are Thy words, O Christ, Eternal Truth, although not all spoken at one time, nor written in one place.

And because they are Thy words and true, they ought to be received by me with thankfulness and faith.

They are Thine, and Thou hast uttered them; and they are also mine, for Thou didst deliver them for my salvation.

I gladly receive them from Thy mouth, that they may be the more deeply engraven upon my heart.

Words of so great tenderness—so full of sweetness and love—kindle my desires; but my offences make me afraid, and a polluted conscience drives me back from the reception of so great Mysteries.

The sweetness of Thy words allures me, but the multitude of my sins weighs me down.

2. Thou commandest me to approach Thee confidently, if I would have part with Thee; and to receive the food of immortality, if I desire to obtain eternal life and glory.

'Come,' Thou sayest, 'unto Me, all ye that labour and are heavy laden, and I will refresh you.'

O sweet and loving word in the sinner's ear, by which Thou, O Lord my God, invitest the poor and needy to the Communion of Thy most holy Body!

But who am I, O Lord, that I should presume to approach unto Thee?

Behold the Heaven of heavens cannot contain Thee, and Thou sayest, 'Come all unto Me.'

3. What does this most gracious condescension, this so friendly invitation, mean?

How shall I dare to come, when I am conscious that there is no good in me, trusting to which I may draw near?

How shall I bring Thee into my house, when I have so often offended Thy most gracious Face?

Angels and Archangels stand in awe of Thee, the Saints and the just fear Thee, and Thou sayest, 'Come ye all unto Me.'

For unless Thou, O Lord, didst say it, who would believe it to be true? and unless Thou didst bid us come, who would ever attempt to draw near to Thee?

4. Behold Noah, a just man, laboured a hundred years in making the ark, that he with a few others might be saved; and how can I in one hour prepare myself to receive with reverence the Maker of the world?

Moses, Thy servant, Thy great and especial friend, made an ark of incorruptible wood, and lined it with the purest gold, that he might lay up in it the tables of the Law; and shall I, a foul creature, dare so lightly to receive Thee, the Framer of the Law, and the Giver of life?

Solomon, the wisest of the Kings of Israel,

built in seven years a magnificent Temple to the praise of Thy Name; and celebrated a feast of dedication for eight days; he offered a thousand peace-offerings, and solemnly brought in the Ark of the Covenant with the sound of trumpets and with shouts of joy unto the place which was fitted to receive it.

And I—miserable and most worthless of men—how shall I bring Thee into my house, I who can hardly even spend half an hour properly in prayer? And would that for once I could spend but half an hour rightly!

5. O my God, how did they strive to please Thee in their actions!

Alas, how little it is that I do, how short a time do I spend in preparing myself for Communion!

Seldom am I wholly recollected, very seldom entirely free from distraction.

Yet surely in the life-giving presence of Deity no unbecoming thought should arise; nor should any creature occupy my mind; for it is not an Angel, but the Lord of Angels, Whom I am going to receive as my Guest.

6. There is, moreover, a vast difference between the Ark of the Covenant with its relics, and Thy most pure Body with its unspeakable virtues; between those legal sacrifices—which were figures of things to come—and the True

Victim of Thy Body, the fulfilment of all ancient sacrifices.

7. Why then do I not burn more with desire for Thy adorable Presence?

Why do I not prepare myself with greater care to take Thy Holy Things? whereas those holy Patriarchs and Prophets of old, Kings also and Princes, with the whole people, shewed such great devotion towards Thy divine service.

8. David—most devout King—danced before the Ark of God with all his might, calling to mind the benefits bestowed in time past upon the fathers; he made instruments of different kinds; he composed psalms, and appointed that they should be chanted joyfully, and he himself also often sung them to the harp, when he was inspired by the grace of the Holy Ghost. He taught the people of Israel to praise God with their whole hearts, and with one harmonious voice to bless and praise Him every day.

If such devotion was then displayed, and such a memorial of divine praise was made before the Ark of the Covenant, how much devotion and reverence should I and all Christian people preserve in the presence of the Sacrament, in the reception of the most precious Body of Christ?

9. Many run to various parts to visit relics of Saints, and wonder when they hear of their achievements; they behold the vast dimensions

of their churches, and kiss their bones, which are wrapt in silk and gold; and behold, Thou art Thyself here present with me on the Altar— my God, the Holy of Holies, the Creator of men, and the Lord of Angels!

Often in sight-seeing there is nothing but human curiosity and the love of novelty, and little practical result comes from it; especially is this the case, when people lightly go from place to place without any real contrition.

But here, in the Sacrament of the Altar, Thou art wholly present, my God and man, Christ Jesus; here an abundant fruit of eternal salvation is granted, as often as Thou art worthily and devoutly received.

But to this there is no attraction for levity, curiosity, or for the senses; but only for faith, devout hope, and sincere charity.

10. O God, Unseen Creator of the world, how wonderfully dost Thou deal with us! how sweetly and graciously dost Thou order all things for Thine elect, to whom Thou offerest Thyself to be received in this Sacrament!

For this surpasses all comprehension; this especially draws the hearts of the devout, and kindles their affections.

For those are truly Thy faithful ones who are always aiming at amendment of life, and who increase in devotion and the love of virtue by frequently receiving this most precious Sacrament.

11. O wondrous and hidden grace of the Sacrament, which the faithful of Christ alone know, but which unbelievers and servants of sin cannot experience.

In this Sacrament spiritual grace is conferred, and the virtue which was lost is repaired in the soul, and the beauty which sin had disfigured returns again.

So great sometimes is this grace, that from the abundance of the devotion here given, not only the mind, but the frail body also is conscious that it has received an increase of strength.

12. Yet we must lament and grieve exceedingly over our lukewarmness and negligence, that we are not drawn with greater affection to receive Christ, in Whom all hope—and all the merit of those who are to be saved—is placed.

For He is our sanctification and redemption; He is the solace of the wayfarers, and the eternal fruition of the Saints.

It is therefore much to be regretted, that many give such little thought to this saving Mystery, which gladdens Heaven, and preserves the whole world.

Alas, the blindness and hardness of the human heart! that it does not more tenderly consider so unspeakable a gift, but from daily use sinks into utter disregard of it.

13. For if this most holy Sacrament were celebrated in one place only, and were consecrated by only one priest in the world, with what desire, think you, would men be affected towards that place, and towards such a priest of God, that they might see the Divine Mysteries celebrated?

But now many are made priests, and in many places Christ is offered; that the grace and love of God to man might appear so much the greater, the more widely the sacred Communion is spread throughout the world.

14. Thanks be to Thee, O good Jesus, eternal Shepherd, Who hast deigned to refresh us, poor exiles, with Thy precious Body and Blood; and to invite us to partake of these Mysteries, even with words uttered by Thine own lips, saying, "Come unto Me all ye that labour and are heavy laden, and I will refresh you."

CHAPTER II.

That the great Goodness and Love of God are made manifest to Man in this Sacrament.

1. TRUSTING in Thy goodness and great mercy, O Lord, I draw near, as one

sick to the Saviour, as one hungry and thirsty to the Fountain of Life, one needy to the King of Heaven, a servant to my Lord, a creature to my Creator; one desolate to my kind Comforter.

But whence is this to me, that Thou deignest to come to me? who am I, that Thou shouldest offer Thyself to me?

How should a sinner dare to appear before Thee? and how dost Thou vouchsafe to come unto a sinner?

Thou knowest Thy servant, and art aware that in him there is no good thing, to entitle him to this favour.

I confess, therefore, my vileness; I acknowledge Thy goodness; I praise Thy tenderness; I give Thee thanks for Thy exceeding love.

From Thyself Thou doest this—not on account of my merits—that Thy goodness may be the better known to me, Thy love more abundantly poured forth, Thy condescension more perfectly displayed.

Since therefore this pleases Thee, and hast been so ordered by Thee, Thy gracious condescension pleases me also; and would that my iniquity may place no obstacle to Thy designs!

2. O most sweet and most gracious Jesus, what great reverence and thanksgiving, with unceasing praise, is due to Thee, for the reception of

Thy sacred Body, whose dignity no man can express.

But what shall I think of in this Communion, in this approach to my Lord, Whom I am unable duly to honour, and yet Whom I devoutly desire to receive?

What can I think of more profitable and more salutary than to abase myself entirely in Thy presence, and to exalt Thy infinite goodness above me?

I praise Thee, my God, and I exalt Thee for ever; I despise myself, and cast myself down before Thee into the depths of my own vileness.

3. Behold, Thou art the Holy of Holies: and I—the scum of sinners!

Behold, Thou bendest Thyself down to me, who am unworthy to look up unto Thee!

Behold, Thou comest to me, Thou desirest to be with me, Thou invitest me to Thy Feast.

Thou desirest to give me heavenly food to eat, even the Bread of Angels, no other indeed than Thyself, the Living Bread, Which camest down from Heaven and givest life unto the world.

4. Behold whence love proceeds! what condescension shines forth! how great should be our thanksgivings and praises for such mercies!

O how salutary and profitable was Thy counsel, when Thou didst institute it! how sweet and pleasant the feast, when Thou gavest Thyself for food!

O how wonderful is Thy working, O Lord, how mighty is Thy power, how infallible Thy truth!

For Thou didst speak and all things were made; this, too, was done at Thy command.

A wonderful thing it is, and worthy of faith, and surpassing man's understanding, that Thou, O Lord my God, true God and man, shouldest be wholly contained under the form of a little bread and wine, and shouldest be eaten by the receiver and yet remain unconsumed.

5. Thou, O Lord of all, Who standest in need of no one, hast desired to dwell by Thy Sacrament in us.

Preserve my heart and body pure from all stain of sin, that with a joyful and clean conscience I may be able very often to celebrate Thy Mysteries, and to receive to my eternal salvation what Thou hast principally ordained and instituted for Thine honour and perpetual memorial.

6. Rejoice, my soul, and give thanks to God, for so noble a gift and so singular a comfort left unto thee in this vale of tears.

For as often as you repeat this Mystery, and receive the Body of Christ, so often do you perform in Act the work of Redemption, and become a partaker of all the merits of Christ.

For the love of Christ is never diminished, and the greatness of His propitiation can never be exhausted.

Therefore you ought always to dispose yourself for this by a new preparation of mind, and with attentive consideration to ponder the great mystery of Salvation.

So great, so new, so sweet it ought to seem to you, each time when you celebrate or when you are present at the Holy Sacrifice, as if on that very day Christ first descended into the womb of the Virgin and was made man, or hung on the Cross, and suffered and died for the salvation of mankind.

CHAPTER III.

That it is Profitable to Communicate often.

1. BEHOLD, I come to Thee, O Lord, that through Thy gift I may receive a blessing, and that I may be gladdened at Thy Holy Feast, which Thou, O God, hast of Thy goodness prepared for the poor.

Behold, in Thee is all that I can desire, or should desire; Thou art my Salvation, and Redemption, my Hope and Strength, my Honour and Glory.

Rejoice, therefore, to-day the soul of Thy

servant, for unto Thee, O Lord Jesus, do I lift up my soul.

I desire now to receive Thee devoutly and reverently; I long to bring Thee into my house, so that, like Zaccheus, I may be worthy to be blessed by Thee, and to be reckoned amongst the children of Abraham.

My soul and my flesh thirst for Thee, my heart desires to be united to Thee.

2. Give Thyself to me, and it is enough; for besides Thee no comfort is of avail. Without Thee I cannot exist, and without Thy visitation I cannot live.

Therefore it behoves me often to draw near to Thee, and to receive Thee as the remedy for my soul's health; lest perchance I fail by the way, if I be deprived of this heavenly sustenance.

For so Thou, most merciful Jesus, preaching to the people, and curing various diseases, on a certain occasion didst say—'I will not send them home fasting, lest they faint by the way.'

Deal with me, therefore, in the same way, for Thou hast left Thyself in this Sacrament for the comfort of the faithful.

For Thou art the sweet refreshment of the soul, and he who shall eat Thee worthily shall be partaker and heir of eternal glory.

3. Indeed it is necessary for me, who so often fall and commit sin, so soon grow lukewarm and

faint, that by frequent prayer, confession, and Holy Communion I should renew, cleanse, and inflame myself, lest perhaps, through deferring too long, I fall away from my holy purpose.

For man's senses are prone to evil from his youth; and unless Divine medicine succour him, he will quickly fall away and become worse than he is.

The Holy Communion, then, draws him back from evil, and strengthens him in good.

For if now I am so often negligent and lukewarm, when I communicate or celebrate; what would become of me, if I did not receive this remedy, and did not seek so great a help?

And although I am not every day fit, nor well disposed to celebrate, yet I will endeavour at stated times to receive the Divine Mysteries, and to render myself a partaker of so great a Grace.

For this is the one principal consolation of the faithful soul, so long as it is absent from Thee in this mortal body; that being mindful of its God, it receives its Beloved One with a devout mind.

4. O wonderful condescension of Thy tender loving-kindness for us, that Thou, O Lord God, the Creator and Giver of life to all spirits, shouldest deign to come to a poor soul, and with Thy whole Deity and Humanity to change its famishing hunger into fatness.

O happy minds and blessed souls which worthily and devoutly receive Thee, their Lord God; and, in receiving Thee, are filled with spiritual joy!

O how great a Lord is received! how beloved a Guest is entertained! how faithful a Friend is welcomed! how beautiful and noble a Spouse is embraced!—one to be loved above all things that are loved, and beyond all that can be desired.

O my Beloved, dearest One! let heaven and earth and all that garnishes them be silent in Thy presence, for whatever of glory or beauty they possess, all is the gift of Thy generosity, and can never reach to the beauty of Thy Name, Whose wisdom is infinite.

CHAPTER IV.

That many Benefits are granted to those who Communicate Devoutly.

1. O LORD my God, prevent Thy servant with the blessings of Thy Goodness, that I may approach worthily and devoutly to Thy magnificent Sacrament.

Stir up my heart towards Thee, and deliver me from this heavy dulness.

Visit me with Thy saving grace, that I may

taste in spirit Thy sweetness, which plentifully in this Sacrament lies hid as in a fountain.

Enlighten, also, mine eyes, to behold so great a Mystery, and strengthen me to believe it with undoubting faith.

For it is Thy operation, and not man's power; Thy sacred institution, not man's invention.

For no one can be found who is able of himself to comprehend and understand these things, which transcend even the finer faculties of Angels.

What part, therefore, shall I, an unworthy sinner, dust and ashes, be able to search into or comprehend of so high and hidden a Mystery?

2. O Lord, in the simplicity of my heart, in a good and firm faith, and at Thy commandment, I draw near to Thee with hope and reverence; and I do sincerely believe that Thou art here, God and man, present in this Sacrament.

Thou desirest, then, that I should receive Thee, and unite myself to Thee in love.

Wherefore I implore Thy clemency, and beseech Thee to grant me special grace for this; that I may be wholly dissolved in Thee and overflow with Thy love, and no longer admit any other consolation.

For this most high and precious Sacrament is the health of soul and body, the remedy of all spiritual languor; by which my vices are cured, my passions are curbed, my temptations are conquered or weakened, greater grace is infused, virtue begun is increased, faith is confirmed, hope is strengthened, and charity inflamed and expanded.

3. For Thou hast bestowed, and still frequently dost bestow, many good things in this Sacrament to Thy beloved servants who communicate devoutly, O my God, Upholder of my soul, Repairer of human infirmity, and Giver of all inward consolation.

For Thou impartest to them much consolation against their various trials, and liftest them up from the depths of their own dejection to the hope of Thy protection; and with a certain new grace Thou dost inwardly revive and enlighten them; so that those who at first felt themselves before Communion distressed and without affection, afterwards, being refreshed with the heavenly food and drink, found themselves changed for the better.

And in this way Thou dost arrange Thy dealings with Thine elect, in order that they may truly own and clearly experience how great is their own infirmity, and how much goodness and grace they obtain from Thee.

For of themselves they are cold, dry, and indevout; but of Thee they are made to become fervent, devout, and full of energy.

For who can humbly draw near to the fountain of sweetness, and not take away some little sweetness?

Or, who can stand by a large fire without gaining from it some little heat?

And Thou art a Fountain always full and overflowing; Thou art a Fire always burning and never failing.

4. Wherefore, if I am not able to draw from the fulness of the fountain nor to drink my fill, I will yet put my mouth to the opening of this Heavenly pipe, that I may receive from it at least some small drop to allay my thirst, that I may not be wholly dried up.

And if I cannot yet be altogether heavenly, nor so inflamed as Seraphim and Cherubim, yet I will try to apply myself to devotion, and to prepare my heart to obtain if it be but a small spark of the Divine fire, by the humble partaking of this life-giving Sacrament.

And whatever is wanting to me, O good Jesus, most holy Saviour, do Thou kindly and graciously supply for me; for Thou hast vouchsafed to call all unto Thee, saying,—'Come unto Me all ye that labour and are heavy laden, and I will refresh you.'

5. I indeed labour in the sweat of my brow, I am racked with grief of heart, I am burdened with sins, I am disquieted with temptations, I

am entangled and oppressed by many evil passions; and there is none to help me, none to deliver and save me, but Thou, O Lord God, my Saviour, to Whom I commit myself and all that is mine, that Thou mayest guard me and bring me to eternal life.

Receive me for the praise and glory of Thy Name, Thou Who hast prepared Thy Body and Blood for my food and drink.

Grant me, O Lord God of my salvation, that by frequenting this Thy Mystery, the fervency of my devotion may increase.

CHAPTER V.

Of the Dignity of the Sacrament, and of the Priesthood.

1. IF you had the purity of an Angel, and the sanctity of St. John Baptist, you would not be worthy to receive, or to handle this Sacrament.

For this is not due as the reward of human merit, that a man should consecrate and handle the Sacrament of Christ, and receive for his food the bread of Angels.

Grand is this Mystery; and great is the dignity of priests, to whom that is given which is not granted to Angels.

For only priests, validly ordained in the Church, have the power of celebrating and consecrating the Body of Christ.

The priest indeed is the minister of God, and uses the Word of God by the command and institution of God; but God is therein the chief Author and invisible Worker, to Whose will all is subject, and Whose behests all obey.

2. You ought to trust Almighty God in this most excellent Sacrament, more than your own senses or any visible sign.

And therefore with fear and reverence you must approach this work.

Take heed to yourself, and see what this ministry is, which has been committed by the laying on of the Bishop's hand.

Behold, you are made a priest, and consecrated to celebrate the Sacrament; see now that you offer this Sacrifice to God faithfully and devoutly in due time, and that you shew yourself blameless.

You have not lightened your burden, but you have now bound yourself by a stricter bond of discipline, and are under the obligation of leading a higher life of sanctity.

The Priest ought to be adorned with all virtues, and to afford to others the example of a good life.

His conversation should not be in accordance

with that of the common and ordinary run of men, but with that of Angels in Heaven, or of perfect men on earth.

3. The Priest arrayed in the sacred vestments is Christ's representative, so that suppliantly and humbly he may pray to God for himself and for all the people.

He has before him and behind him the sign of the Cross of his Lord, that he may continually bear in mind Christ's Passion.

Before him he bears the cross on the chasuble, that he may diligently look at the footsteps of Christ, and fervently endeavour to tread in them.

Behind him he bears on his back the cross, that he may meekly endure for God's sake any trials which others may bring upon him.

He bears the cross before him, that he may bewail his own sins; and behind him, that he may compassionately weep for the sins of others, and that he may know that he is appointed to stand between God and the sinner, and that he may not grow weary in prayer and holy oblation, till he prevail to obtain grace and mercy.

When a priest celebrates the Sacrament, he honours God, he gladdens the Angels, he edifies the Church, he helps the living, he obtains repose for the dead, and renders himself partaker of all good things.

CHAPTER VI.

An Enquiry as to the Way to prepare for Communion.

1. WHEN I consider Thy dignity, O Lord, and my own vileness, I tremble exceedingly, and am confounded within myself.

For if I do not come unto Thee, I fly from life; and if I intrude myself unworthily, I incur Thy displeasure.

What then am I to do, my God, my Helper and Adviser in troubles?

2. Teach Thou me the right way; suggest to me some short spiritual exercise, suitable before Holy Communion.

For it is profitable to me to know how indeed I should devoutly and reverently prepare my heart for Thee, for a healthful reception of Thy Sacrament, or also for celebrating so great and divine a Sacrifice.

CHAPTER VII.

Of the Examination of our own Conscience, and of the Resolution to Amend.

1. ABOVE all things it behoves God's priest to come to celebrate, handle, and re-

ceive this Sacrament, with the deepest lowliness of heart and suppliant reverence, with full faith and dutiful intention for the honour of God.

Examine diligently your conscience, and to the best of your power cleanse and brighten it by true contrition and humble confession; so that you may not have upon it, or be conscious of, any weighty matter, which may be a cause of remorse, and hinder your free approach.

Let all your sins in general be hateful to you, and especially grieve and lament for your daily transgressions.

And if time will allow, lay bare before God in the secret of your heart all the miseries which spring from your passions.

2. Sigh and grieve that you are yet so carnal, and worldly, and your passions so unmortified.

That you are so full of corrupt inclinations, so unguarded in your outward senses; so often ensnared by many vain imaginations.

So much inclined to outward things, so negligent as to inward.

So ready for laughter and dissipation, so unready for weeping and compunction.

So prompt for relaxation and bodily comfort, so disinclined for austerity and fervour.

So curious to hear news, and see fine sights, so slack to embrace what is lowly and common.

So eager to have much, so sparing in giving, so close in retaining.

So inconsiderate in speech; so unable to keep silence.

So undisciplined in manners, so impetuous in actions.

So greedy about food, so deaf to the Word of God.

So hasty to take rest, so slow to labour.

So wakeful to listen to stories, so sleepy at holy vigils.

So anxious to finish devotions, so wandering in attention.

So careless in saying the hours, so lukewarm in celebrating, so dry in communicating.

So soon distracted, so rarely fully recollected.

So suddenly stirred to anger, so apt to take offence.

So ready to judge, so relentless in reproving.

So joyful in prosperity, so weak in adversity.

So often making good resolutions, so seldom bringing them to good effect.

3. These and other defects being confessed and deplored with sorrow and with great displeasure at your own weakness, make a firm resolve ever to amend your life, and more and more to advance in virtue.

Then with full resignation, and with your whole will, offer yourself up to the honour of

My Name, on the altar of your heart, as a perpetual burnt-offering; faithfully committing to Me your body and soul, that thus you may be worthy to approach to offer the Sacrifice to God, and to receive to your health the Sacrament of My Body and Blood.

4. For there is no more worthy oblation, nor satisfaction greater for washing away sin, than to offer yourself purely and wholly to God, together with the oblation of Christ's Body at Celebration and at Communion.

If a man does what lies in his power, and is truly penitent, as often as he draws near to Me for pardon and grace—'as I live,' saith the Lord, 'who will not the death of a sinner, but rather that he be converted and live, I will not remember his sins any more, but they shall all be forgiven him.'

CHAPTER VIII.

Of the Oblation of Christ on the Cross, and of Resignation of Ourselves.

1. AS I freely offered Myself with outstretched hands and naked Body upon the Cross to God the Father for thy sins, so that nothing remained in Me which was not

turned into a sacrifice of Divine Propitiation; so ought you also to offer yourself voluntarily to Me daily at the Celebration of the Divine Mysteries, with all your strength and affections —to the utmost of your spiritual power.

What do I require of you more, than that you should strive to resign yourself entirely to Me?

Whatever you give besides yourself, I do not care for, for I seek not yours, but you.

2. As it would not satisfy you, if you possessed everything but Me; so neither can it please Me, whatever you give, if you withhold yourself.

Offer yourself to Me, and give yourself wholly to God, and your offering shall be accepted.

Behold I offered Myself without reserve to the Father for you; I have also given you My whole Body and Blood for your food, that I might be wholly yours, and you might be Mine to the end.

But if you stand on self, and do not freely offer yourself to My will, the oblation is not complete, neither will there be entire union between us.

Therefore all your works should be preceded by the voluntary offering of yourself into the hands of God, if you desire to obtain freedom and grace.

For this is the reason why so few are enlightened, and made inwardly free, because they cannot deny themselves without reserve.

My sentence stands firm,—'Unless a man forsake all, he cannot be My disciple.'

If you therefore wish to be My disciple, offer yourself to Me with all your affections.

CHAPTER IX.

That we ought to Offer Ourselves and all that we have to God, and to Pray for All.

1. O LORD, all things are Thine which are in heaven, and in earth.

I desire to offer myself to Thee as a free-will offering, and to remain Thine for ever.

O Lord, in the simplicity of my heart, I offer myself to Thee to-day, to be Thy servant for ever, to obey Thee, and to be a sacrifice of perpetual praise.

Receive me together with this holy oblation of Thy precious Body, which I offer to Thee this day in the presence of the Angels—who are invisibly assisting; that it may be for the salvation both of myself and of all Thy people.

2. O Lord, I offer to Thee all my sins and offences, which I have committed before Thee and Thy holy angels, from the day in which I was first capable of sin even to this hour, on Thy

propitiatory altar; that Thou mayest both consume them and burn them with the fire of Thy love, and blot out all the stains of my sins, and purify my conscience from every fault, and restore to me Thy grace, which by sin I lost—fully pardoning me for all, and receiving me mercifully to the kiss of peace.

3. What can I do in respect of my sins, but humbly confess and bewail them, and incessantly entreat Thy propitiation?

Hear me graciously, I beseech Thee, when I stand before Thee, my God.

All my sins are most displeasing to me, I desire never to commit them any more, but I grieve for them, and will grieve for them as long as I live; I am ready to do works of repentance, and to make satisfaction to the best of my power.

Forgive me, O God, forgive me my sins, for the sake of Thy Holy Name.

Save my soul, which Thou hast redeemed with Thy precious Blood.

Behold, I commit myself to Thy mercy, I resign myself into Thy hands; deal with me according to Thy Goodness, and not according to my wickedness and iniquity.

4. I offer also to Thee all my good works—however poor and imperfect they may be—that Thou mayest amend and sanctify them, that they may please Thee and be rendered accept-

able to Thee, and be made better and better; and that Thou mayest bring me, a slothful and unprofitable creature, to a happy and blissful end.

5. I offer also to Thee all the pious desires of devout persons; the necessities of parents, friends, brothers, sisters, and of all who are dear to me, and of all who for love of Thee have been benefactors to me or others; or, who have asked and desired me to pray and offer the Holy Sacrifice for themselves and all theirs— whether they are now living in the flesh, or already have departed; that all may experience the help of Thy grace, the aid of Thy consolation, protection from dangers, and deliverance from future pains; and that, being rescued from all evils, they may with joyfulness pay Thee a glorious tribute of thanksgiving.

6. I offer to Thee also propitiatory prayers, for those especially who have in any way injured, grieved, or reproached me, or caused me any harm or annoyance.

And I offer also for all those whom I have in any way grieved, vexed, oppressed, and scandalized, by word or deed, knowingly or unknowingly; that Thou mayest equally forgive us all our sins, and all our offences against each other.

Take away, O Lord, from our hearts all suspiciousness, indignation, anger and contention, and whatever is calculated to wound charity, and to lessen brotherly love.

Have mercy, O Lord, have mercy on those who seek Thy mercy; give grace to the needy; make us so to live, that we may be found worthy to enjoy the fruition of Thy grace, and may attain to eternal life. Amen.

CHAPTER X.

That the Holy Communion is not for a Slight Thing to be Abstained from.

1. YOU ought frequently to have recourse to the Fountain of grace and of Divine mercy—to the Fountain of goodness and of all purity; so that your passions and vices may be healed, and that you may be worthy to be rendered more strong and watchful against all the temptations and deceits of the Devil.

The Enemy, knowing how great is the fruit and remedial force which is laid up in the Holy Communion, does every thing in his power by all means and occasions to hinder and restrain devout and faithful persons from approaching it.

2. For when some are preparing themselves for Holy Communion, they suffer from worse assaults and suggestions of Satan than at other times.

The Evil Spirit himself, as Job relates, comes amongst the sons of God to disturb their minds according to his usual malice, or to make them scrupulous and perplexed; so that he may diminish the warmth of their affections, or by an assault undermine their faith, or perchance may get them to abstain from Communion altogether, or to approach it without fervour.

But we must pay no regard to his wiles and suggestions, however shameful and horrible they may be, but hurl back all such imaginations on his own head.

The wretch should be despised and scorned, and no one should ever abstain from Holy Communion, because of his assaults, or the inner conflicts he stirs up.

3. Often also our over-anxiety to feel devotion, and a certain uneasiness about our confession, are hindrances.

Follow the counsel of the wise, and lay aside anxiety and scruple, because such check the grace of God, and destroy devotion.

For some small fall or trouble do not abstain from Holy Communion, but go quickly and confess it, and freely forgive all who have offended you.

But if you have offended any one, humbly beg pardon, and God will freely forgive you.

4. What is the good of delaying for a long

time your confession, or of putting off Holy Communion?

Purge yourself as soon as possible, spit out the poison quickly, hasten to receive the remedy, and you shall feel better than if you had delayed a long while.

If to-day you defer for this, perhaps to-morrow you will have a greater obstacle; and so for a long time you may be hindered from Communion, and become more and more unfit.

As quickly as possible shake off your present vexation and sluggishness; for it is no good to go on long in anxiety and distress of mind, and on account of daily obstacles to abstain from receiving the Divine Mysteries.

Indeed, it is most hurtful to delay Communion for a long time, for delay produces a deadness of soul.

Alas, some lukewarm and self-indulgent persons are glad of an excuse for delaying confession, and are desirous too of deferring Holy Communion, in order that they may not feel obliged to preserve a stricter watch over themselves.

5. Ah! what little love, what feeble devotion, have those who thus readily postpone Holy Communion!

How happy is he and how acceptable is he to God, who so lives, and preserves such a purity of conscience, that even every day he is fit and well-disposed to communicate, if it were granted him, and if it might be done without observation of others.

If a person sometimes abstains out of humility, or because of some legitimate hindrance, his feeling of reverence is to be commended.

But if a spirit of indifference have crept over him, he must stir himself up, and do all he can, and the Lord will assist his desire for a good will—for that He specially looks to.

6. But when he is lawfully hindered, he will always have the good desire and pious intention of communicating, and so will not lack the fruit of the Sacrament.

For the devout soul may any day or hour profitably and without hindrance draw near to Christ in spiritual communion.

And yet on certain days, and at the stated times, the Body and Blood of his Redeemer ought to be sacramentally received with affectionate reverence, and the praise and glory of God should be set above the thought of his own consolation.

For he spiritually communicates and is invisibly refreshed, as often as he does devoutly recall the Mystery of Christ's Incarnation and Passion, and is inflamed with the love of Him.

7. But he who does not prepare himself,

unless when a great festival is at hand, or when custom obliges, will too often be unprepared.

Blessed is the man who offers himself as a burnt-offering to the Lord, as often as he celebrates or communicates.

Do not be too long nor too rapid in celebrating, but between the two observe the happy medium of those with whom you live.

You ought not to cause others annoyance and weariness, but to keep the ordinary way, which was appointed by our forefathers; and rather consider the profit of others, than your own devotion or feelings.

CHAPTER XI.

That the Blessed Sacrament and the Holy Scriptures are most necessary to the Faithful Soul.

1. O MOST sweet Lord Jesus, how great is the sweetness of the devout soul that feasts with Thee in Thy banquet; there no other food is placed to be eaten but Thyself—the One alone Beloved, and more to be desired than all that the heart can desire!

To me, indeed, it would be sweet to be able in Thy Presence to pour forth tears from inmost affection, and with the devout Magdalen to wash Thy feet with my tears.

But where is this devotion? where this flood of holy tears? Surely in Thy sight, and in that of Thy holy Angels, my heart ought to burn and to weep for joy.

For I possess Thee truly present in this Sacrament, though veiled under another form.

2. For to behold Thee as Thou art in Divine Brightness, my eyes could not endure; neither could the whole world abide in the splendour of the Glory of Thy Majesty.

In this, therefore, Thou accommodatest Thyself to my weakness, by thus hiding Thyself under the Sacrament.

I truly possess and adore Him Whom Angels in Heaven adore; but I as yet in faith, they indeed by sight and without a veil.

I must be content with the light of true faith, and walk in it, until the Day of eternal brightness break, and the shadows of figures pass away.

But when that which is perfect is come, Sacraments will no longer be needed, because the Blessed in celestial glory will require no sacramental medicine.

For they rejoice without end in the presence of God, beholding His glory face to face; and being transformed from brightness to brightness in the abyss of Deity, they taste the Word of God made flesh, as He was from the beginning, and as He remaineth for ever.

3. When I picture these wonders, even my spiritual comforts, whatever they may be, become tedious to me and heavy; and as long as I do not gaze on my Lord in His glory, I count as nothing all that I see and hear in this world.

Thou art my witness, O my God, that nothing is able to give me consolation, nor any creature to give me rest, but Thou only, my God, Whom I desire eternally to contemplate.

But this is not possible during this mortal life; and therefore I must exercise great patience, and submit myself in every desire to Thee.

For Thy Saints also, O Lord, who now rejoice with Thee in the Kingdom of Heaven, whilst they lived on earth, waited with faith and much patience for the coming of Thy glory.

What they believed, I believe; what they hoped for, I hope for; and where they have attained, I trust by Thy grace also to come.

In the meanwhile I will walk by faith, strengthened by the examples of the Saints.

I have also holy books for my comfort, and a mirror of life; and above all, Thy most holy Body for my special remedy and refreshment.

4. For I feel that two things are most of all necessary to me in this life, without which this

miserable life would become to me insupportable.

Whilst detained in the prison of this body, I confess that I have need of these two things, namely, food and light.

Therefore Thou hast provided for my weakness by giving Thy sacred Body, for the refreshment of my mind and body; and Thou hast set Thy Word as a light unto my feet.

Without these two I could not well live; for the Word of God is the light of my soul, and Thy Sacrament is the Bread of life.

These may be called the two tables—set on this side and on that side—in the treasury of Thy Holy Church.

One table is that of the Holy Altar, having the sacred bread, that is, the precious Body of Christ; and the other is that of the Divine Law, containing holy doctrine, teaching the right faith, and leading securely even into that within the veil, where is the Holy of Holies.

5. Thanks to Thee, O Good Jesus, Light of Eternal Light, for the table of holy doctrine, which Thou hast delivered to us by Thy servants the Prophets, Apostles, and other Teachers.

Thanks to Thee, Creator and Redeemer of mankind, Who to declare Thy love to the whole world hast prepared a great supper, in which, not the typical lamb, but Thy most sacred Body and Blood are set before us to be eaten—rejoicing all the faithful with this holy Feast, and inebriating them with the cup of salvation, in which are all the delights of Paradise; and the holy Angels too join us in this Feast, and with a sweetness more blessed than ours.

6. O how great and honourable is the office of Priests, to whom it is given to consecrate with sacred words the Lord of Majesty; to bless with their lips, to hold Him in their hands, to take Him into their mouth, and to administer Him to others!

O how clean ought those hands to be, how pure the mouth, how holy the body, how spotless the heart of the Priest, into whom so often the Author of purity enters.

From the Priest's mouth, which so often receives the Sacrament of Christ, nothing should proceed but what is holy, virtuous and edifying.

7. His eyes should be simple and chaste, which are accustomed to behold the Body of Christ.

The hands should be pure and raised towards Heaven, which are wont to handle the Maker of Heaven and earth.

To the Priests especially in the law it is said, 'Be ye holy, for I the Lord your God am holy.'

8. May Thy grace assist us, O Almighty God, that we, who have undertaken the priestly office,

may be enabled worthily and devoutly to serve Thee, in all purity and good conscience.

And if we cannot live in such innocency of life as we ought, yet grant us duly to weep for the sins we have committed; so that, in the spirit of humility, and with the full purpose of a good will, we may be enabled to serve Thee more fervently for the future.

CHAPTER XII.

That he who is about to Communicate ought to use Great Diligence to prepare himself for Christ.

1. I AM the Lover of purity, and the Giver of all sanctity.

I seek a pure heart, and there is the place of My rest.

Make ready for Me a large upper room furnished, and I will eat the passover at thy house with My disciples.

If you desire Me to come to you, and to abide with you, purge out the old leaven, and cleanse the habitation of your heart.

Shut out all the world, and all the tumult of evil passions; sit as a sparrow 'alone upon the house-top,' and reflect upon your misdeeds in the bitterness of your soul.

For every lover prepares for the dearly beloved one the best and most beautiful place, for in this way is made known the affection which is entertained for the beloved.

2. Know then that you cannot make a sufficient preparation by the merit of your own actions, even if for a whole year you should prepare yourself and give no thought to anything else.

But out of My mere goodness and favour you are suffered to approach My Table, in the same way as a beggar may be invited to the banquet of a rich man, and would have nothing else to return him for his benefits, but to humble himself and give him thanks.

Do all in your power, and do it diligently, not out of custom nor necessity, but with fear, reverence, and affection, receive the Body of thy beloved Lord God Who deigns to come to you.

I am He Who called you, I have commanded it to be done, I will supply what is wanting to you. Come and receive Me.

3. When I grant the grace of devotion, give thanks to God; for you are not worthy of it, but I had compassion on you.

If you have no devotion, but rather feel yourself dry, be instant in prayer, sigh, smite yourself, and do not desist until you have gained some crumb or drop of saving grace.

You have need of Me, I have no need of you.

Neither do you come to sanctify Me, but I come to sanctify and better you.

You come that you may be sanctified from Me, and united to Me; that you may receive some fresh grace from God, and be anew stirred up to amendment of life.

Do not neglect this grace, but always prepare your heart with all diligence, and take into thee thy Beloved.

4. But it behoves you not only to prepare yourself before Communion, but also carefully to keep up the spirit of devotion, after you have received the Sacrament.

Watchfulness is not less required afterwards, than devout preparation before.

For a good guard over yourself after receiving is the best preparation for gaining greater grace in a future Communion.

If a man at once gives himself unrestrainedly to outward comforts, he will be thereby rendered exceedingly indisposed to spiritual things.

Beware of talking much, remain in secret, and enjoy your God; for you possess Him, Whom all the world cannot take from you.

I am He, to Whom you ought to give yourself wholly, so that you may live already no longer in yourself, but in Me,—free from all anxiety.

CHAPTER XIII.

That with the whole Heart the Devout Soul ought to seek Union with Christ in the Sacrament.

1. WHO, O Lord, will grant me this, that I may find Thee alone, that I may open my heart to Thee, that I may enjoy Thee as my soul desires; and that none may look upon me, nor any creature move me, nor have regard to me; but that Thou alone mayest speak to me, and I to Thee, as lover speaks to lover, and friend feasts with friend?

This I pray for, this I desire, that I may be united wholly to Thee, and that I may detach my heart from all created things, and that through the Holy Communion and frequent Celebrations I may more and more learn to taste celestial and eternal things.

Ah, Lord God, when shall I be wholly united to and absorbed in Thee, and altogether unmindful of myself?

'Thou in me, and I in Thee;' and so grant that this mutual indwelling may be abiding!

2. Truly Thou art my Beloved, the Choicest amongst thousands, in Whom my soul is well pleased to dwell all the days of my life.

Truly Thou art my Peace-maker, in Whom is

the highest peace and true repose; out of Whom is naught but labour, sorrow, and endless misery.

'Verily, Thou art a God that hidest Thyself,' and Thy counsel is not with the wicked, but Thy converse is with the humble and simple.

O how sweet is Thy spirit, O Lord, Who to shew Thy goodness to Thy children, dost vouchsafe to refresh them with that most delightful bread which comes down from Heaven.

Truly there is no other nation so great, which 'hath God so nigh unto them,' as Thou, our God, art to all Thy faithful; to Whom, for their daily comfort, and to lift up their hearts to Heaven, Thou givest Thyself to be eaten and enjoyed.

3. For what other nation is so illustrious as the Christian people? or what creature under heaven so beloved as the devout soul, to whom God comes, that He may feed it with His own glorious Flesh?

O unspeakable grace! O wonderful condescension! O boundless love, bestowed singularly on man!

But what shall I render to the Lord for this grace, for love so remarkable as this?

There is nothing that I can give more acceptable to Him, than to offer my heart entirely to my God, and to be intimately united to Him.

Then all that is within me shall rejoice, when my soul shall be perfectly joined to God.

Then will He say to me, 'If you desire to be with Me, I desire to be with you.'

And I will reply to Him, 'Condescend, O Lord, to abide with me, I will gladly stay with Thee.'

'This is my whole desire, that my heart may be united to Thee.'

CHAPTER XIV.

Of the Ardent Desire of some Devout Persons for the Body and Blood of Christ.

1. O HOW plenteous is Thy Goodness, O Lord, which Thou hast secretly laid up for those that fear Thee!

When I call to mind, O Lord, with what devotion and affection some devout souls draw near to Thy Sacrament, then I am very often confounded and ashamed that I approach Thy Altar and the Table of Holy Communion with so much indifference and coldness; that I remain so dry and indevout and heartless; that I am not wholly inflamed in Thy Presence, my God, nor so vehemently drawn and affected as many devout souls have been, who from excessive desire and the actual feeling of love were unable to restrain themselves from weeping, but with the mouth of heart and body alike have panted with their inmost being after Thee, O God, the Fountain of life; who were unable otherwise to allay or satisfy their cravings, unless by receiving Thy Body with all delight and spiritual avidity.

2. O truly ardent faith of theirs, existing as a fit proof of Thy sacred Presence!

For they really know their Lord in the breaking of bread, when their hearts so mightily burned within them from the fact that Jesus walked with them.

Alas, such affection is often far from me, and such devotion and mighty fervour.

Be merciful to me, O good Jesus, sweet and gracious; grant to Thy poor suppliant, sometimes to feel some little of that warm affection of love in the sacred Communion; that my faith may be more strengthened, my hope in Thy goodness increased, and that my love, once thoroughly kindled, when the Heavenly Manna has been tasted, may never fail.

3. But Thy mercy is able to give me the grace I desire, and to visit me most benignantly with the spirit of fervour, when the day of Thy good pleasure shall arrive.

For although I do not glow with such great desire as those who have a special devotion to

Thee, yet through Thy grace I have the desire to obtain their more ardent desire, and I pray and desire to be made partaker with all Thy fervent lovers, and to be numbered with their holy company.

CHAPTER XV.

That the Grace of Devotion is obtained by Humility and Self-Denial.

1. IT is necessary that you should seek the grace of devotion instantly, that you ask for it earnestly, that you wait for it patiently and trustingly, that you receive it thankfully, that you preserve it humbly, that you carefully co-operate with it; and that you commit to God the time and manner of the heavenly visitation, until He shall please to come to you.

You ought chiefly to humble yourself when you feel little or no inward devotion; but not to be cast down, nor to give way to undue sadness.

God often gives in one short moment what He has withheld for a long time.

And sometimes at the end of the prayer He grants, what in the commencement He delayed to give.

2. If always grace were at once given, and

came at the wish for it, it would be more than feeble man could well bear.

Therefore the grace of devotion must be waited for, with good hope and humble patience.

Ascribe it, however, to yourself and to your sins, when it is not given, or when it is secretly withdrawn.

Sometimes it is a little thing which hinders or hides the grace; if, indeed, any thing can be called little, and not rather great, which is an obstacle to so great a good.

But if you will put away this thing—whether it be little or great in itself—and completely overcome it, you will have what you have sought.

3. For as soon as you have given yourself up to God with your whole heart, and no longer seek this or that for your own will and gratification, but place yourself entirely in His hands, you will find that you are united and at peace; because nothing will then delight and please you, so much as the good pleasure of the Divine Will.

Whoever, therefore, in simplicity of heart raises his intention up to God, and rids himself of all inordinate love or dislike of any created thing, he will be most fit to receive grace, and be most worthy of the gift of devotion.

For the Lord gives His blessing there, where

He finds the vessels empty; and the more completely any one renounces the things below, and the more he by contempt of himself dies to self, so much the more speedily grace comes, the more copiously does it flow in, and the higher does it lift up the heart which has been set at liberty.

4. Then shall he 'see and flow together, and' his 'heart shall fear and be enlarged' within him, because the hand of the Lord is with him, and he has placed himself wholly in His hand—even for ever.

Behold, thus shall the man be blessed, who seeks God with all his heart, and does not receive his soul in vain.

This man, when he takes the Holy Eucharist, obtains a great grace of Divine union; because he does not look to his own feeling of devotion and consolation, but to the glory and honour of God.

CHAPTER XVI.

That we ought to lay open our Necessities to Christ, and to seek His Grace.

1. O MOST sweet and loving Lord, Whom I now desire devoutly to receive, Thou knowest my infirmity, and the wants I suffer; in

how great evils and corrupt passions I am involved; how often I am weighed down, tempted, disturbed and stained with sin.

I come to Thee for help, I entreat of Thee consolation and relief; I speak to Thee, Who knowest all things, to Whom my whole inner life is manifest, and Who alone can perfectly comfort me and succour me.

Thou knowest what good things I stand most in need of, and how poor I am in virtues.

2. Behold, I stand before Thee poor and naked, asking for Thy grace, and imploring Thy mercy.

Refresh a suppliant hungering at Thy doors, inflame my coldness with the fire of Thy love, enlighten my blindness with the brightness of Thy presence.

Turn all earthly things into bitterness for me, all things painful and adverse into occasions of patience, all things earthly and created into contempt and oblivion.

Lift up my heart to Thee in Heaven, and do not suffer me to wander upon earth.

Mayest Thou alone begin to be sweet to me, from this moment for evermore; for Thou alone art my food and my drink, my love and my joy, my delight and all my good.

3. O that Thou wouldest thoroughly inflame me with Thy presence, consume and trans-

form me into Thyself; that I might be made one spirit with Thee, through the grace of inward union, and the meltings of ardent love!

Suffer me not to go from Thee, empty and dry; but deal with me mercifully, as Thou hast often dealt wonderfully with Thy Saints.

What wonder is it if I should be wholly set on fire by Thee, and all self disappear; since Thou art a Fire always burning and never going out, a Love purifying the heart, and enlightening the understanding.

CHAPTER XVII.

Of Ardent Love for, and Vehement Desire to receive Christ.

1. WITH the greatest devotion and burning love, with all affection of heart and fervour, I desire to receive Thee, O Lord, as many Saints and devout persons—who were most pleasing to Thee from their holiness of life, and who were most fervent in devotion—desired Thee, when they communicated.

O my God, Eternal Love, all my good and boundless happiness, I would gladly receive Thee with the most vehement longing, and the most profound awe, that any of the Saints ever had, or could experience.

2. And although I am unworthy of any of these feelings of devotion, yet I offer to Thee the whole affection of my heart, as if I were the only one who had all these delightful, ardent longings.

But whatever a pious mind is able to conceive and desire I present and offer to Thee, with the deepest reverence and inmost fervour.

I wish to reserve nothing for myself, but to sacrifice spontaneously and most gladly myself and all that is mine to Thee.

O Lord my God, my Creator and my Redeemer, I desire to receive Thee to-day with such affection, reverence, honour and praise, with such gratitude, worthiness and love, with such hope, faith and purity, as Thy most holy mother, the glorious Virgin Mary, possessed, as she received and desired Thee, when the Angel announced to her the Mystery of the Incarnation, and she humbly and devoutly answered—'Behold the handmaid of the Lord, be it unto me according to Thy word.'

3. And as Thy blessed Forerunner—most excellent among Saints—John Baptist, rejoicing at Thy presence, leapt for joy, whilst he was yet enclosed in his mother's womb; and, afterwards, when he beheld Jesus walking among men, he humbled himself greatly, and with devout affection said, 'The friend of the bridegroom that standeth and heareth him, rejoiceth greatly be-

cause of the bridegroom's voice;' so also do I long to be inflamed with great and holy desires, and to present myself to Thee with my whole heart.

Wherefore also I offer and present to Thee the rejoicings of all devout hearts, the ardent affections, the mental raptures, the supernatural lights and celestial visions, with all virtues, and praises that are or shall be celebrated by all creatures in Heaven and earth, for myself, and for all commended to my prayers; that thus Thou mayest be worthily praised by all, and glorified for ever.

4. Receive my vows, O Lord my God, and my desires to render Thee infinite praise and boundless blessing, such as are justly due to Thee, according to the greatness of Thy unspeakable majesty.

These I render to Thee, and desire to render to Thee, every day and every moment of my life; and I call upon and invite all heavenly spirits and all faithful people, by prayers and affections, to unite with me in rendering thanksgivings and praises to Thee.

5. Let all people, tribes, and tongues praise Thee, and with highest devotion and thrilling joy let them magnify Thy holy and delicious Name.

And may all who reverently and devoutly celebrate, and receive with full faith, Thy most august Sacrament, be worthy to find grace and mercy with Thee; and let them earnestly pray for me, a sinner.

And when they have obtained the devotion which they desired and blissful union, and have departed from the sacred heavenly Table, fully comforted and wonderfully refreshed, let them vouchsafe to remember me, a poor creature.

CHAPTER XVIII.

That a Man should not be a curious Searcher into the Sacrament, but a Humble Follower of Christ, submitting his senses to the Sacred Faith.

1. YOU ought to avoid all curious and profitless searching into this most profound Sacrament, if you do not desire to be plunged into depths of doubt.

'He that is a searcher of My Majesty, shall be overpowered by its glory.'

God is able to do more than man's mind can understand.

A pious and humble investigation of the truth is tolerated, provided we are always ready to be instructed, and desire to walk according to the wholesome doctrine of the Fathers.

2. Blessed is the simplicity, which avoids difficult questions, and walks on the plain and firm footpath of the commandments of God.

Many have lost devotion, because they would search into deep matters.

Faith is required of you, and an upright life; not depth of intellect, and subtle knowledge of the Mysteries of God.

If you do not understand, nor receive into your mind the things beneath you, how will you comprehend the things which are above you?

Submit yourself to God, and humble your sense to faith, and the light of knowledge shall be given to you, so far as shall be necessary and good for you.

3. Some are sorely tempted as to their faith in the Sacrament; but this is not to be ascribed to themselves, but rather to the enemy.

Do not trouble about those thoughts, nor dispute with them, nor make answer to the doubts which the Devil instils; but believe the words of God, believe His Saints and Prophets, and the wicked enemy will fly from you.

The servant of God often profits much by suffering such things.

For the Devil does not tempt unbelievers and sinners, whom he already holds securely; but he tempts and harasses devout believers in various ways.

4. Go forward, therefore, with simple and unhesitating faith, and with sincere reverence approach the Sacrament; and whatever you

cannot understand, commit safely to Almighty God.

God does not deceive you; he is deceived who trusts too much to himself.

God walks with the simple; He reveals Himself to the lowly; He gives understanding to little ones; He discloses His meaning to pure minds, and hides His grace from the curious and proud.

Human reason is weak and fallible, but true faith cannot be deceived.

5. All reasoning and investigation by natural means ought to follow, not precede, nor intrude into the domain of, faith.

For faith and love in this most holy and most sublime Sacrament must here especially take the lead, and work by hidden ways.

God, Who is eternal, incomprehensible, and of infinite power, does great and unsearchable things in Heaven and on earth, and His wonderful works are 'past finding out.'

If the works of God were of such a nature as to be easily comprehended by human reason, they could neither be called wonderful nor 'unsearchable.'

Library of Spiritual Works
English Catholics

IT is hoped that the "Library of Spiritual Works for English Catholics," which will comprise translations, compilations, and other works, will meet a need which has long been felt. As the devotional life of the Church of England has increased, so the demand for spiritual treatises has become more and more urgent, and has arisen from all classes of society. This series of books, some well-known, some already oftentimes translated, and others, it may be, yet to be presented for the first time in an English dress, is intended to meet this want.

The aim of the translators is twofold. First, to provide the reader with a fair rendering of the original as far as possible unmutilated. It has been a common complaint of late, that translations have been marred by the absence of parts of the original, the exclusion of which a more intelligent view of Catholic devotion in the present day has rendered unnecessary. In these editions these omissions have been to a great extent supplied; yet at the same time any term or expression which may come under the imputation of being "un-English" has been reduced, as far as may be without destroying the thought, to its equivalent in Anglican phraseology and belief. Secondly, to translate the original into ordinary English, and thus to avoid the antiquated and stilted style of writing, which often makes books of this kind distasteful, or even sometimes unintelligible.

IN SMALL 8VO, ELEGANTLY PRINTED WITH RED BORDERS ON EXTRA SUPERFINE TONED PAPER, CLOTH EXTRA, RED EDGES,

PRICE 5s. EACH.

Of the Imitation of Christ.

In Four Books.　By THOMAS À KEMPIS.

[*Now ready.*

The Spiritual Combat.

By LAURENCE SCUPOLI.　　[*Nearly ready.*

The Devout Life.

By S. FRANCIS DE SALES.　[*Nearly ready.*

Other Works are in Preparation.

THESE EDITIONS ARE PREPARED ESPECIALLY FOR THIS SERIES.

RIVINGTONS

London, Oxford, and Cambridge

RIVINGTONS

London .... *Waterloo Place*
Oxford .... *High Street*
Cambridge ... *Trinity Street*

www.ingramcontent.com/pod-product-compliance
Lightning Source LLC
Chambersburg PA
CBHW030733230426
43667CB00007B/696